A HAMLYN POINTER BOOK

HOW BIRDS BEHAVE

A HAMLYN POINTER BOOK

HOW BIRDS BEHAVE

By Neil Ardley

Illustrated by David Andrews

HAMLYN

LONDON · NEW YORK · SYDNEY · TORONTO

The illustrations in this book have been
selected from the Hamlyn all-colour paperback
BIRD BEHAVIOUR by John Sparks

Cover illustration by Ken Lilly

First published 1971
Second impression 1972
Published by The Hamlyn Publishing Group Limited
London · New York · Sydney · Toronto
Hamlyn House, Feltham, Middlesex, England
© Copyright The Hamlyn Publishing Group Limited 1971
ISBN 0 600 34361 8
Printed by Officine Grafiche Arnoldo Mondadori,
Verona, Italy.

contents

Page

BIRDS CAN BE FASCINATING

Apart from the icy Poles and summits of very high mountains, there is probably no place on Earth that has never been darkened by the shadow of a bird. Most of us see birds every day and, although we probably spot only a few of the 8,600 different kinds or species, they are important to us. We keep birds as pets; we stalk them with binoculars and cameras – and hunt them with guns; we feed them on our bird tables – and eat their meat and eggs; and we may even wear their feathers as decoration.

Animals that move gracefully are always more interesting to watch than animals that do not, and birds move in the most fascinating way of all – they fly. People can only dream of flying through the air by themselves, and a flying dream is usually an exhilarating experience. When we watch birds flying so easily through the air, we secretly envy them, and this is perhaps why birds are one of the most popular of all groups of animals.

Birds also interest us because of their dependence on vision, a dependence that we share with them. Like humans, birds use their eyes to find out about

Above: The Tawny Owl, like all owls, has huge eyes that enable it to hunt at night.

Left: Brown Harrier Eagles use their eyes to spot their prey from great heights, before swooping down to capture their victims.

Right: Chaffinches and a House Sparrow escaping from a cat. The way in which birds behave often means the difference between life and death for a bird. Birds that are able to take wing as soon as they spot an enemy approaching will live and breed. But birds that react slowly will probably soon be caught and die. Most birds will behave in the same way regardless of whether the approaching animal is friendly or unfriendly. But some birds, such as pigeons in public squares, learn to change their natural behaviour when it is to their advantage.

Below: The Mockingbird of North America is one of the world's best singers. It is one of several birds that people admire for their beautiful voices.

the world around them. Most animals live in a world of smells, and use their noses to hunt their prey and identify their fellows. We have all seen our pet dog or cat investigate something new with its nose – not the way we would go about it! But birds use their eyes to find their food and to detect each other as we do. And, like us, they behave in special ways towards each other. They make colourful displays that are attractive and interesting to watch. Birds also use sound in a meaningful way and their voices, from the comical mimicry of parrots and mynah birds to the beautiful song of the canary and the nightingale, amuse us and charm us.

These are some of the types of bird behaviour that fascinate us. What is also interesting is *why* birds should behave in the way that they do.

BEHAVIOUR IS IMPORTANT

From the moment it hatches from its egg, the way in which a bird behaves is vital to its life. It needs food, warmth and protection from its parents, and it must act in the correct way to get them. Once it leaves the nest, a bird must find its own food and shelter, and keep itself clean. It must avoid enemies, and will probably seek a mate in order to breed. Its life will never be easy. Failure usually means death and a bird's survival will depend on whether it behaves correctly at the right moment.

7

Many of a bird's actions have direct survival value. Birds escaping from a pouncing cat are behaving in a way to keep alive. In a very different way, but with the same purpose, a bittern among reeds will freeze if an enemy comes near and stay absolutely still, so that it will not be spotted. Both kinds of behaviour have evolved by *natural selection*. That is, the birds which survive are those that are best at survival behaviour, and this survival ability is handed down to their offspring. Each of a bird's behaviour patterns, evolved over many generations, helps it to survive in some way or other.

Above: A Great Tit is able to use its feet and bill in a complicated way to get at a morsel of food on the end of a piece of string. It pulls up half the string with its beak, and holds it in place with its feet. In this way, the food is raised high enough for the tit to take it in its bill. Such behaviour does not come automatically, but has to be learned by the bird. Tits can learn to use their bills and feet in clever ways, because this type of behaviour comes naturally to them and suits their way of life. A chaffinch, for example, would find it hard to learn such a trick because it does not normally use its bill and feet together to feed.

KINDS OF BEHAVIOUR

Birds behave in many different ways all the time, but their actions can be grouped into two types. One type of behaviour keeps the bird itself alive and well and does not affect other birds very much. Such actions include flying, feeding and cleaning, and these activities are called *maintenance activities*. The other type of behaviour is social, or how a bird acts towards other birds – how it "talks" to another bird or makes another bird react in some way. These social activities are called *displays*. Behaving in the correct way towards others is very important in large groups of birds, just as obeying the law is important to us if we want to live together peacefully.

Displays may consist of groups of set movements carried out like rituals, or of various unusual postures.

They may look absurd to us, but each has an exact meaning to the birds involved.

Ethologists, scientists who study behaviour, have to look carefully at the situations in which displays happen. A display by a male bird on a nesting site may mean it wants a mate; but it may also mean that the bird is warning other males to keep away from its nesting site.

RED RAG TO A ROBIN

Some kinds of actions are caused by signals. A robin is a very aggressive bird when it has territory to defend, and will attack any strange robins that enter its own territory. If a bunch of red feathers is placed in the territory, the robin will attack the feathers as savagely as any rival. It is thought that the red breast of the strange robin acts as an attacking signal to the first robin, and so he attacks.

This kind of behaviour exists among humans. Advertisements bombard us with signals to make us behave in such a way as to want to buy their products.

LEARNING HOW TO BEHAVE

Many of a bird's actions are inherited and instinctive. Young birds can fly as soon as they leave their nests. However, they do not always fly well right away, and often have to "practise" flying before they become perfect. Much behaviour has to be learned, and as it goes through life a bird picks up all sorts of information that influences its actions. Finding the best place to roost; knowing what is good to eat and what isn't and where to find food; which birds to avoid and which to bully – these are types of behaviour that a bird can only learn from experience. Unlike human behaviour, which is almost all learned, bird behaviour is part learned, part instinctive.

Below: Young swallows can fly as soon as they leave the nest, and so they obviously do not have to learn to fly. But their flying ability improves with experience as they get older.

KEEPING CLEAN

Washing and bathing may often seem to be a chore, but think how much worse it would be if you were a bird and covered with thousands of feathers. Even a bird the size of a sparrow has between 2,000 and 3,000 feathers to deal with. These feathers are important. They trap a layer of air next to the skin which helps to keep the bird warm and, in water birds, to float. They enable the bird to fly, and even help it to communicate with other birds! Keeping all the feathers clean and in working order is essential to a bird's life, and cleaning behaviour is very important.

It doesn't take long for the plumage to become soiled and need cleaning. It quickly gets dirty with pollen, mud and dust, and parasites such as fleas and lice often live among a bird's feathers, chewing them and sucking the bird's blood.

TAKING A BATH

Most birds like to take a bath regularly. If they are stopped from doing so in captivity, they become very unhappy and will jump into some water as soon as they are released. The water helps to remove dirt from the feathers, and probably helps the bird in preening its feathers after bathing.

Several kinds of birds like to bathe together. The sight of one bathing will make the others want to join in. Robins will often crowd into the water together and splash around and enjoy themselves. With these birds, bathing is an infectious occupation, and it serves to keep a flock together. This is useful, because the chances of survival are better in flocks.

Above: A Goldfinch washes itself by first tipping its body forward into some water, thrashing its bill about and flicking its wings up and down (top). Then it rests back on its tail and moves the wings to and fro across the back in a "scissoring" motion. In this way the water is splashed over the bird's feathers (bottom).

Left: A group of Bronze-winged Manakins rest flank-to-flank along a branch and preen each other. Birds that sit together like this are called *contact species* because they are often in contact.

Left: A Kingfisher washes itself by plunging into the water from the air. This is one of the easiest ways of getting the feathers wet before the bird sets about preening. Birds that spend much of the time in flight wash by plunging. These birds include swifts, terns and drongos. The plunge probably helps to dislodge some dirt from the feathers. Preening with the beak then serves to recondition the feathers for flying, and to remove parasites such as fleas and mites from the plumage.

The methods of bathing vary. Water birds have only to dip down below the surface, sometimes turning a somersault, to get wet all over. They then rub their heads along their sides and wings. Most land birds bathe by standing in shallow pools of water and spreading out their feathers to let the water penetrate. But others, such as babblers, jump in and out of the water over and over again. Some birds, especially larks, bathe in the rain. Parrots and hornbills spread out their feathers to get wet, whereas we put up umbrellas to stay dry! Some birds do not bathe in water at all, but prefer dust baths to clean themselves. Grouse, pheasants, and turkeys are dust bathers.

Left: A Song Thrush becomes dirty and dishevelled when it does not preen properly.

PREENING

A bath in water is not enough to get the plumage into perfect condition again. Just as women use creams and lotions to condition their skin, birds use a special oil to restore their feathers. This oil is a waxy substance and is contained in an oil gland beneath some feathers on the bird's back. After shaking and fluttering its wings to get rid of the water left from bathing, the bird turns its head, wipes its beak to

Above: Male and female Oriental White-eyes preen each other.

Above: A male Mallard obtains oil from its oil gland for preening. The gland is usually covered by overlapping feathers. The oil gland is very important to water birds such as ducks, because the oil helps to make the feathers repel water. If the oil gland is removed, the condition of the duck's plumage deteriorates.

Left: House Sparrows take dust baths to clean themselves! They scratch little holes in the soil and sift dust through their feathers to remove fleas and mites.

Above: A female Cuban Finch preens a male, which raises its feathers to invite preening.

Right: A Jay "anting". Anting is a strange method of cleaning that at least 160 kinds of birds use. The Jay sits with its feathers fluffed out over some ants, and allows them to stream over its body. The ants squirt formic acid, which may act as an insecticide to kill parasites.

clean it, and then, with its beak, takes some oil from the oil gland. It then smears the oil over the feathers. This is called *preening*. The wing feathers come first, because the bird must restore its full powers of flight as soon as possible. Then the rest of the body is preened. Finches take as long as 20 minutes to preen.

Oiling is especially important to water birds because it helps to waterproof the feathers. We talk about water rolling off a duck's back, and it is the oil on the feathers that causes this to happen. The oil

may also be important to a bird's health. In sunshine, the oil produces vitamin D, and this prevents a disease called rickets.

Sometimes the oil is coloured and used like cosmetics! Some gulls and terns apply rose-coloured oil to their breasts in the breeding season, and the yellow oil of the Great Hornbill is smeared on its wings.

A few birds do not have an oil gland. These are ostriches, emus, cassowaries, frogmouths and bustards, among the land birds, and, oddly enough, those great fishermen, the cormorants.

Several kinds of birds like to preen each other, rather as monkeys do. One bird preens the feathers of the bird sitting next to it, often in answer to a special preening invitation. The invitation may consist of ruffling up the feathers, or of facing away so that the neck is presented to a neighbour. This social preening, or *allopreening,* is particularly useful in dealing with head feathers. There are 38 families of birds, from penguins to crows, which preen one another. Many of them are birds that sit side by side or share small nest sites, such as noddies, fairy terns and razorbills.

HEAD SCRATCHING

The head obviously cannot be preened with the bill. If the bird does not have a companion to do it for him, then he has to scratch instead. Most birds scratch *directly*, with the leg under the wing. But some birds scratch *indirectly*, with the leg brought over the wing. Most passerine or perching birds, turacos, swifts, hummingbirds, hoopoes, oystercatchers, avocets and stilts scratch in this way. Some birds, such as wood warblers and parrots, use both methods.

Scratching is very important to birds that fish to get food, such as herons. These birds spend much time standing in water and their feathers become soiled with slime. The usual cleaning methods are of little use, and herons have patches of downy feathers that produce a fine powder. They "comb" this powder over their feathers with their claws, and it soaks up the slime.

Above: A Starling uses its bill to apply some ants to its feathers. No-one knows for sure why birds use ants. Anting may help to keep the feathers in good condition, it may kill parasites such as fleas and mites, it may relieve itching or it may just feel pleasant.

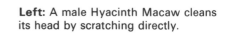

Left: A male Hyacinth Macaw cleans its head by scratching directly.

Above: A Red Avadavat (a small grass-finch of India) preens itself after bathing. It first wipes its beak to clean it (1), and then takes oil from its oil gland (2). The oil is smeared over the bill and then transferred to the feathers. The avadavat draws its primary wing feathers through its bill to preen them (3), but other wing feathers are preened by twisting the head backwards (4). The neck is easily bent so that the rump feathers can be reached (5), but the tail has to be twisted to get to the vent (6). The wing is spread to preen underwing feathers (7). The whole procedure takes at least 10 minutes.

Left: A male Bullfinch scratches indirectly – it brings one leg over its lowered wing.

FINDING FOOD AND DRINK

Eating and drinking are as important to birds as they are to us, for we and they, like all animals, soon die without food or drink. But, in some ways, eating and drinking are even more important to a bird than to a human. As they fly, birds use up immense amounts of energy to keep their wings flapping. They get this energy from their food and drink, and must therefore eat large quantities of food just to keep going. Hummingbirds, which hover in the air by moving their wings to and fro very rapidly, burn up amazing quantities of energy. If a man could work at the rate that a hummingbird has to work, he would have to eat as much as twice his own weight in food every day to get enough energy. And he would have to drink almost his own weight in water every hour just to keep cool!

Few birds use as much energy as hummingbirds, but life for all birds is a constant search for food, especially in winter. Tits have to find a morsel of food of average size every $2\frac{1}{2}$ seconds for nine-tenths of the day during the winter. Wood pigeons search for food for 95 per cent of the daylight hours. If these birds did not work so hard at finding food, they would starve.

Birds eat all kinds of food, from the tiny algae (one-celled plants) that flamingos take from the salt water of the East African lakes where they live, to the monkeys that are the favourite dish of eagles in the

Above: Greenfinches drink by lowering their heads into a pool and taking up some water in their beaks. Then they raise their heads into the air and tip the water back down their throats, just like a person gargling. Most birds drink in this way.

Left: A Jay is startled by the appearance of a moth and flies away instead of eating it. The moth resembles the bark of a tree when its wings are folded, but when its wings are spread open, they reveal two strange eye-spots. The spots look so much like eyes that the bird thinks it is attacking a large animal and not a moth, and it flies away in alarm without eating the moth. Insects are very likely to be eaten at migration time, when birds have to eat a lot in preparation for their long flights.

Right: A pigeon drinks by putting its beak into a pool or a puddle and sucking up some water. This is a very unusual way to drink – few birds behave in this way. Some grassfinches that live in deserts suck up water, for it is a better way to drink if water is scarce.

Philippines. Many birds eat insects. They will turn over leaves, dig into the soil, probe into the bark and trunks of trees – in fact, do almost anything to find tasty insects. Some birds even follow large animals, which stir up insects as they move about. Birds of prey, such as eagles, kites and owls, live on small mammals such as mice and rabbits, snakes and other reptiles, some insects and even small birds. Sea birds and water birds catch fish and other water creatures such as crabs and water snails. Many other kinds of birds prefer plants to animals. Perching birds, such as finches, eat nuts and seeds, and a fifth of the world's birds live mainly on nectar from plants. Most nectar-eating birds live in South America.

Right: The type of seeds that a bird eats depends on the size and strength of its beak. The Linnet, which has a light and delicate bill, eats large amounts of small seeds such as millet seed (top). The Chaffinch prefers medium-sized seeds such as hemp seeds, as its bill is not strong enough to handle large seeds (centre). The Greenfinch has a strong bill and eats small amounts of large seeds, such as sunflower seeds (bottom). Birds with light bills will eat large amounts of small seeds that they can open quickly, rather than struggle to open large seeds.

Above: The Skimmer's beak (1) acts like a trap. The beak is opened and the lower mandible (jaw) slices through the water. When it touches something to eat, down comes the top mandible like a mouse trap. The Flamingo (2) can strain plankton from the water with special fringes in its sieve-like bill. Both the Hawaiian Honeycreeper (3) and Puff-legs Hummingbird (4) have long, thin beaks to probe down into flowers and reach the nectar.

Eating from plants is easier in some ways than eating animals, which will put up a fight and try to escape being eaten. Some animal-eating birds get round this difficulty by eating dead animals, or carrion. Vultures are famous for eating carrion. A few birds will even steal food from other birds. The Bald Eagle often lays an ambush for Ospreys returning with the fish they have caught. The eagle, the stronger bird, is able to attack the Osprey in mid-air and get it to drop its fish. Then the Bald Eagle dives down and catches the fish before it hits the ground or water below. Along the Atlantic coast of America, Laughing Gulls will raid Brown Pelicans, and steal some of the fish that the pelicans have caught in their great pouch-like bills.

DRINKING

Obtaining water in some way is essential to all birds, in order to replace the water they lose from their bodies. In the Antarctic, penguins get water by eating snow, but elsewhere birds drink. They drink in several ways. Birds that spend most of their time in the air will swoop down to a lake or stream and scoop up water in their beaks. Other birds prefer to drink on the ground, standing by the water and lowering their heads to drink. A few birds, especially

Above: Hawfinches (5) and Crossbills (6) have large strong beaks for cracking open seeds. The Hawfinch can even open a cherry stone. The Nightjar (7) lives on insects. Its weak bill opens wide and the bristles around it help to catch insects. Geese, such as the White-fronted Goose (8), have bills with saw-like edges to crop grass.

Above: Most birds of prey have hooked beaks to tear at their prey, but the rare Everglade Kite uses its beak to get water snails out of their shells.

pigeons, suck up the water in much the same way as we drink through a straw. But most birds take some water in their bills, and then tip their heads back to let the water run down their throats.

Birds eat instinctively from the time they are born. Many birds also seem to have a built-in set of directions that help them to find the right food. But they may also have to learn where the best food is found and catching it successfully often takes a good deal of practice. Drinking, too, does not always seem to be instinctive, and birds may have to learn to recognize water and to drink it. Some types of food contain more water than others. A bird living on juicy insects, for instance, gets more water in its food than a bird that lives on seeds.

BEAKS, BEAKS, BEAKS

Birds have all kinds of beaks or bills, from the great colourful jaws of the toucan and strange paddles of the spoonbill to the elegant tweezers of some hummingbirds and the little forceps of the sparrow. But however strange it looks, a bird's beak is the right shape and size to enable the bird to get the food it wants.

Birds with little beaks, such as the robin and other members of the thrush family, use their beaks simply to grasp food before swallowing it. They catch insects, especially the grubs or larvae, and worms in their beaks, as well as lots of plant food, particularly fruit. Fruit-eating birds, like robins, have been known to gorge themselves on over-ripe cherries and get slightly drunk!

Above: The Huia is an extinct bird of New Zealand. The male Huia (1) and female Huia (2) had different beaks and so could eat different kinds of food. The male uncovered insects, while the female probed holes for them. The Great Spotted Woodpecker (3) has a beak like a chisel for uncovering insects that bore holes into wood. The Red-breasted Merganser (4) has a beak with saw-tooth edges to grip the slippery fish that it captures.

Many birds have long, thin bills which they use as probes, chisels, or spears. Hummingbirds have probing bills with which they seek out the nectar in flower heads, and wading birds, such as herons, often use their bills to probe about on the bottom under the water, seeking fish, frogs, and other water creatures. A woodpecker has a chisel-like beak to gouge away the bark of a tree and dig down into the wood in search of wood-boring insects. Once it comes across its victims, it gets them out by darting its long tongue down the holes they have bored. Oyster-catchers use their long, thin beaks like chisels to attack partly-open oyster shells and get at the molluscs inside. Kingfishers and several other water birds use their sharp beaks like spears to pierce and hold fish.

Some water birds have very strange beaks. The pelican can dive and trap several fish at once in its great pouch-like bill. Some fish-eating birds, such as the Red-breasted Merganser, have bills with saw-tooth edges to help grip their slippery victims. The Skimmer has an unusual way of feeding. It flies over the surface of the water with its large bill open wide

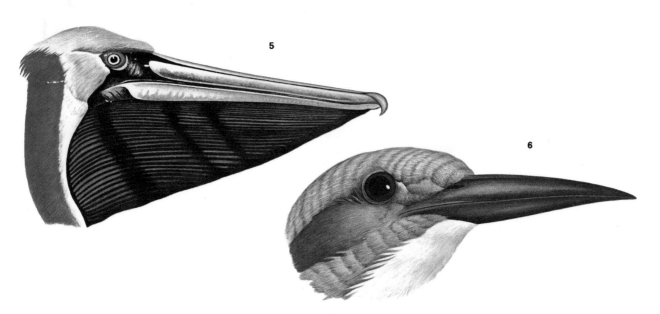

5

6

Above: The Brown Pelican (5)
traps fish inside its pouch-like bill,
but the Common Kingfisher (6)
has a pointed beak with which to spear
fish.

and one mandible, or jaw, just under the water. By ploughing through the water in this way, it can scoop up fish and trap them in its beak. But the flamingo has one of the strangest beaks. These elegant, pink birds stand on thin stilt-like legs at the edges of the lakes, browsing in the mud at the bottom. Their bent bills and their tongues have fringes that act like sieves to strain out minute plants and animals from the mud and water. In fact, a flamingo could not swallow a large piece of food, because its tongue would be in the way!

Often, birds use their beaks to deal with their food in some way besides just grasping it. Seed-eating birds use their beaks to crack open seed kernels and get to the food inside. Many of these birds have strong bills that can open large seeds, and so cut down the number of seeds they need to eat. The Crossbill is a seed-eater with a strange bill like two crossed hooks, which it uses to get seeds out of evergreen cones. Birds of prey use their sharply hooked beaks to tear their prey into pieces before eating.

Beaks may have other uses besides feeding. Parrots have strong, curved beaks that enable them to crack open seeds and bite chunks out of fruits. But anyone who keeps a parrot in a cage knows how it uses its beak to clamber about. Many birds have beaks with colourful markings that serve to identify the sex or species of the bird. The markings are also helpful in feeding young, as we will see later.

Below: The Blue Tit often holds pieces of food in its feet. Tits will also pull branches towards them to help them get at some food. These birds are very deft at using their feet. Tits can be tamed to eat from the hand, and are sometimes trained to perform clever tricks.

Left: The Purple Gallinule can use its feet to pick up pieces of food. This is an unusual way for a bird to feed, for most birds simply grasp their food in their beaks. The Purple Gallinule is a brightly-coloured water bird of the Americas. It lives in marshes as far north as the southern United States and as far south as Uruguay and northern Argentina. It is just over 30 cm long. The Gallinule's feet are not webbed, but its toes are very long and prevent it from sinking into the masses of water plants among which it lives. The toes have flexible joints that enable the bird to grasp pieces of food and pick them up. Gallinules make nests of floating vegetation.

USING THE FEET AND CLAWS

Several birds use their feet as well as their beaks in feeding. Just walking through the grass or bushes may be enough to stir up insects that the bird can then catch. Some herons and other waders will stamp about in shallow water for the same reason.

Birds of prey depend on their feet to get food. A bird of prey first uses its sharp claws or talons to strike its victim, and it will then hold its prey in its talons like meat hooks while it uses its sharp beak to tear the animal apart. Vultures are birds of prey, but they feed mainly on dead animals and so have no need to kill or hold their food. As a result, vultures have weak feet. But some birds are very dexterous in using their feet, especially parrots, owls and tits. Tits can pull up a piece of food on the end of a length of string in order to eat, as shown on pages 8 and 9.

Right: A Short-billed Woodpecker Finch of the Galapagos Islands in the Pacific Ocean uses a spine from a cactus plant. Normally, this finch can use its bill to catch the insects it feeds on. But if the insects it wants are in a deep hole or a crevice and out of reach, it will take a sharp cactus spine or small twig in its beak and probe down inside the hole or crevice. When the insect runs out, the Woodpecker Finch drops the spine and snaps up the insect in its beak. This tool-using ability, which is very rare in birds, is partly instinctive. But the finch probably learns to use the spine or twig more effectively with practice. The Woodpecker Finch belongs to a group of 14 varieties of finches called Darwin's finches, which are found only on the Galapagos Islands. Darwin's study of these finches led to his famous theory of evolution.

Right: An Egyptian Vulture drops a stone on to an ostrich egg to crack it open so that it can eat the contents. This is another example of a bird that can manipulate a tool to get something it wants. The Egyptian Vulture first chooses a heavy stone and picks it up in its beak. Then it walks over to the egg, raises itself up on its toes, and lets go of the stone. Young birds do this instinctively as soon as they see an ostrich egg, but until they have had some practice, they often miss the egg and drop the stone to one side. This shows that part of the behaviour is inborn in that the bird knows what to do, but part is learned in that the bird must learn how to do it correctly.

USING TOOLS

A few types of birds use objects as tools to get at their food. This is unusual and rare behaviour for a bird. The best known tool-using bird is the Short-billed Woodpecker Finch from the Galapagos Islands. This bird eats insects, but it gets them in a very strange way. It breaks off a sharp spine from a cactus, or a small twig from a tree, and holds it in its beak. It then uses this "tool" for probing down holes and crevices in trees and other places where there might be insects. When the insects run out, the finch lets go of the spine or twig and gobbles them up.

Using a tool helps a bird to use an extra source of food which it would otherwise be unable to get at. The Egyptian Vulture uses large stones to crack open ostrich eggs. When the vulture finds an egg, it looks around for a heavy stone and picks up one

Right: A Blackbird looks on as a European Song Thrush breaks open a snail shell on a stone to get at the tasty snail inside. Several birds use natural objects to help them feed. They are not quite as amazing as the tool-users, but it is an unusual way of feeding all the same. Several species of birds get their food out of hard shells by dropping the shells from the air on to rocks or hard ground. Gulls often drop crabs or sea shells to break them open. The Lammergeyer or Bearded Vulture is particularly fond of eating bones. It carries large bones aloft in its talons and drops them on to special dropping areas. The bones crack open and the bird can get at the marrow inside.

in its beak. Then it walks over to the egg, stands over it on tip-toe and drops the stone. In this way, it can get at the tasty yolk inside the egg. In Europe the Song Thrush also uses rocks and stones to open snail shells, but in a different way: it takes a snail in its bill and smashes the shell against a hard rock, called an "anvil". Other birds behave in a similar way. Gulls often drop crabs and sea shells from the air to crack them open and get at the animals inside. A graceful vulture bird called the Lammergeyer has special areas of ground for dropping and cracking open bones, and even tortoises.

Nuthatches and Great Spotted Woodpeckers have a special way of dealing with hard nuts. They ram a nut into a gap in the bark of a tree or a crevice which they have chiselled out with their beaks. The crevice holds the nut tight, and the bird can then split it open with a few hammer-like blows of its beak.

Some bower birds use tools in ways other than for feeding. They adorn their bowers with pigments from plants, using wads of bark or pads of leaves as brushes. Bower birds are shown on pages 50 and 51.

ARE BIRDS INTELLIGENT?

The fact that some birds know how to use a tool to get food might seem to indicate that these birds are highly intelligent, but their behaviour is mainly instinctive. As the bird grows older, it will learn from experience the most effective way to use the tool.

There have been a few cases of bird behaviour which suggest that some birds do use intelligence to get food. A Green Heron was observed to place pieces of bread into a pond to attract fish to the surface. It drove away any birds that came to the bread, and ate the fish that started to nibble the "bait". Then it saw some more fish swimming a few feet away, and put some more bread out as bait. This behaviour is no different from the way a fisherman catches fish, and it appeared that the heron knew exactly what it was doing.

In Finland during the winter, men fish through holes in the ice. They leave baited lines in the water to catch the fish. Once, a crow discovered how to pull in the lines by grabbing a line in its bill and walking away from the hole. Then it put down the line, walked back along it to stop the line sliding back, and pulled up some more until it got the fish on the end of the line. This was certainly an intelligent thing to do.

Above: A Grey Jay stores seeds, such as acorns, and pieces of meat in a tree. It sticks the food into its hiding place with its own saliva. The jay has special enlarged saliva glands to help it store food in this way. It fills its beak and throat with the food, then flies into the woods to hide it all away. Most birds that store food hide it beneath the ground. But the Grey Jay lives in North America where deep snow covers the ground in winter, and so has to store its food somewhere above the ground. But even if the food does become covered with snow, the jay can usually remember where it is and will find it again without difficulty.

Scientists have experimented with birds of the crow family and found that they are capable of solving complicated tricks or puzzles to get food. In the wild, they will look for other sources of food if one source runs out. Less intelligent birds would not think to look elsewhere and would therefore starve.

STORING FOOD

Birds often starve in the winter when there is little food about. Many people know this and put out crumbs of bread and other food to help keep them alive. Some birds are not in need of such help, because they store food during the summer and autumn when it is plentiful and live on their hoards during the winter. Shrikes make larders of food by impaling beetles, lizards and nestling birds on thorns, but they do not need to store this food for long because they migrate for the winter.

Food that is stored for the winter, however, is very important for the survival of birds, and some birds are very adept at storing. In North America, Acorn Woodpeckers live in small communities and bore holes in certain trees. They store acorns in the holes, and can get many thousands of acorns into one tree. Birds of the crow family are good hoarders. In an oak wood in England, about 30 jays were

Right: The Thick-billed Nutcracker finds a hidden store of hazel nuts that it has buried beneath the snow. This nutcracker lives in Scandinavia, where the winters are very cold. During the autumn, when the hazel nuts ripen in the lowlands, the nutcrackers fly about filling up their throat pouches with the nuts. The birds then fly off to higher ground not far away, and bury their mouthfuls of nuts in holes in the ground. When winter comes, the nutcrackers can live off their food stores, easily finding them under the snow. Bird watchers in Sweden once kept watch on 351 nut stores throughout the winter. Although the snow was 50 cm deep, the birds came back to nearly nine out of ten stores. Possibly the birds locate the nuts by remembering landmarks such as trees or buildings. The nut stores often last right through into the spring, when the newly-hatched young are fed with nuts stored the previous autumn! The one nut in ten that a bird misses will probably germinate, and a tree may grow there, helping to spread the forest.

Left: A Greater Honeyguide leads a Honey Badger to a bees' nest. In Africa, honeyguides make unusual partnerships with other animals and even men in order to obtain food. These birds are particularly fond of bees and wasps, and have tough skins which may help prevent stings from the insects. They also like the beeswax in the honeycomb in bees' nests, which they are able to digest. But the honeyguide cannot get at the honeycomb without help. By singing and chattering at the top of its voice, it attracts the attention of an animal or a man. Then, fluttering around and flying ahead of its partner, it leads the way to the bees' nest, usually about half a kilometre away. The animal or man digs out the nest to raid the honey, and the honeyguide can then get at the pieces of honeycomb left over. Honeyguides, like cuckoos, lay their eggs in the nests of other birds and never bring up their own young. The young birds' foster-parents cannot teach them to eat wax, and so honey-guides must look for partners by instinct. Scientists call this strange bird *Indicator*, because of its ability to indicate the way to the honey.

observed to bury some 200,000 acorns during the month of October. Although they are good at finding most of these acorns later, even under several inches of snow, they will forget a few. Their forgetfulness actually does Nature a favour by helping the growth of forests, especially uphill where acorns would not naturally be distributed. Birds usually locate about nine-tenths of their hidden food. Some birds will work over an area thoroughly to uncover their hidden stores, but others may use landmarks, such as trees or buildings, to help find it.

HELPING BIRDS TO FEED

Many people help to keep birds alive all the year round by giving them food. But many birds take advantage of people to get food without having such deliberate help. Tits often perch on milk bottles and peck through the foil tops to raid the milk inside. A robin may swoop down and settle near a gardener turning over some soil, ready to gobble up any worms that are dug up. Birds form similar partnerships with

animals. They can find food more easily by associating with other animals than by searching on their own. Cattle egrets often live with herds of cattle, eating the insects and reptiles that the cattle disturb as they feed. In North America, ptarmigans live with caribou for the same reason, and gulls in Alaska associate with brown bears to pick up the remains of the salmon the bears eat.

Right: Cattle Egrets live with oxen. These birds, also called Buff-backed Herons, live in most parts of the world. But wherever they live, they are always to be seen in the company of cattle. They feed on the insects and reptiles stirred up by the cattle as they browse, and can often be seen perching on the backs of their hosts. Zoologists have found that the Cattle Egrets get more to eat in this way than if they have to hunt their prey by themselves. Although they may seem to be clever birds, their behaviour is instinctive and is not learned from others.

Opposite page: A Robin grabs a wriggling worm brought up from under the earth by a man digging. Robins often watch men digging and rush in to snatch up the worms. This is an example of a bird living in partnership with man in order to obtain food. Birds often realize that people will provide them with food, and come to live near them. Gulls follow ships, ready to swoop down and gobble up any tasty bit of garbage thrown overboard by the crew. Partnerships with people are easy for birds. They have to do little more than just wait to be fed.

Some animals expect something in return, and birds in partnerships with these animals have to behave in certain ways to satisfy their partners. In Africa, oxpeckers live with large animals such as oxen, rhinos and giraffes. They sit on their backs and eat the small ticks and flies that infest their hosts' bodies. In this way, the birds can eat and the animals are rid of their troublesome pests.

A bird that forms one of the strangest partnerships is the honeyguide. Honeyguides are small forest birds of Africa and Asia. The African species, especially the Greater Honeyguide, are very fond of the beeswax found in the honeycomb in bees' nests. They are able to digest this wax because they have special bacteria in their intestines. The honeyguide cannot, on its own, open a bees' nest to get at the wax, so it leads an animal, such as a honey badger or a bear, or even a human, to the nest. The animal or man breaks open the nest to take the honey, thus exposing the beeswax, and the bird can eat its fill!

LIVING TOGETHER

The old proverb "birds of a feather flock together" is true for many kinds of birds. Other birds, such as shrikes and most birds of prey, are solitary birds and like to remain alone for most of the year. Birds have to come together to breed, of course, and the breeding season is the only time when many solitary birds meet, either in groups or pairs. But most birds, like humans, are social creatures and prefer to live in each other's company. You have only to visit a city square during the winter to see great flocks of starlings roosting.

Apart from the purpose of breeding, why should most birds want to spend their time together? And why should other birds prefer to go off on their own? Consider the problems that birds are faced with all the time: avoiding enemies and getting food. A bird that lives with many others of the same kind in a flock is less likely to be attacked by an enemy. Its fellow birds will raise the alarm in good time and several birds can work together to drive the attacker away.

A solitary bird has none of these advantages, but many solitary birds have plumage that tends to blend in with the landscape where they live. This camouflage protects the bird from the attentions of its enemies. The Rock Ptarmigan even changes its plumage to suit the season. In summer it is brownish, in autumn it becomes grey, and in winter it turns white! In this way, it always harmonizes with the rocky tundra in the northern wastes where it lives. It matches the low plants of summer, the bare rock of autumn, and the snow of winter.

The kind of food that a bird eats also determines whether it is to be a social bird or a solitary bird. If a lot of its food can be found in a small space, such as berries on a tree, then the birds that eat the berries will flock together. A single tree can provide enough food for the flock, and if the birds can eat without interfering with one another, then they will stay together and trust to safety in numbers. But solitary birds depend on their stealth, speed and skill to get their food. If they hunted in a group, they would disturb each other's prey and no bird would catch anything. This is not always true, however. Insect-eating birds may work together in seeking food. One bird will flush out insects for the others to catch.

Left: A group of Common Starlings resting on a branch space themselves out about 10cm apart. Most social birds sit in rows with each bird just far enough from its neighbour so that one can jab at another if it misbehaves. If they come closer, one bird will threaten or avoid the other. Common Starlings have a beautiful blue-green sheen, and in autumn their feathers grow the striking white tips shown here. They are social birds and often live together in large groups. Starlings come in huge flocks to live in cities during the winter, and will take up residence on ledges of buildings and bridge girders. They can be a great nuisance in cities, and are difficult to remove.

KEEPING ONE'S DISTANCE

Some birds like to sit in huddles, pressed closely together. Most of these birds live in the tropics where it is warm, and enjoy close contact. But in colder parts of the world, some birds huddle for warmth. Wrens, tree creepers, Long-tail Tits and swifts sometimes cluster together at night. Emperor

Right: Skylarks do not always live together in flocks and, in fact, prefer to be on their own for much of the time. Many birds are solitary birds. For protection these birds have plumage that is a similar colour to the land on which they live. Skylarks live in open country, such as grassy plains and treeless moors, and they walk and run along the ground instead of hopping. Their light brown plumage acts as camouflage and protects them from their enemies. It is possible to get quite close to a Skylark on the ground without seeing the bird. However, it will have seen you, and will suddenly fly up into the air, singing sweetly. Skylarks live in Europe, Asia and North Africa. They have been introduced successfully to New Zealand, Hawaii and Vancouver Island in Canada.

Right: A flock of Bohemian Waxwings may rob a bush completely of its berries before the birds fly on to find another bush. Waxwings live together in large flocks. They migrate and stay together during the winter, and they also live in groups when they are breeding. The waxwings like to eat fruit and berries, especially cherries and cedar and juniper berries. Flocks of waxwings wander from place to place in search of fruit, often moving from one area to another as the fruit becomes ripe. Waxwings live in Europe, Asia and North America.

Penguins in the icy Antarctic can, by huddling together, keep down the amount of heat they lose by one-fifth, and save valuable reserves of fat that they have in their bodies.

Most social birds like to sit a little distance from each other. Sitting flank-to-flank makes them irritable, and so they keep just far enough away from each other to be out of range of their neighbours' beaks.

Left: When birds band together to get food, each one has a specific rank and must await its designated turn to feed. The sequence for feeding is called a *peck order*. These four birds have found some crumbs put out for them in snow. The large, dominant Blue Jay (1) eats first, then the Starling (2). Next come the smaller birds, with the Purple Finch (3) dominating the Black-capped Chickadee (4).

Right: Two male Mandarin Ducks and a female go through the motions of drinking as a greeting ceremony to each other. This ceremony occurs among friendly ducks, and such greetings are common to many wild fowl. When birds live together in groups, rituals like this are necessary to keep the birds peaceful. Humans behave in a similar way. We often shake hands with strangers to show that we feel friendly towards them. Sharing food and drink at a cocktail party helps people to talk and be friendly with one another. Birds that live in groups often behave in the same way at the same time, especially when they have to deal with marauding enemies and find food. Mandarin Ducks live in the wild in Eastern Asia and Japan. They are a favourite with people who keep ducks, and can be seen in captivity in many parts of the world.

PECK ORDER

We say that "the early bird gets the worm", but it would be more correct to award the prize to the strongest and most aggressive bird. These birds can bully their fellows in the flock, and get the best perches, the choicest food and the most desirable mates. This principle extends all the way down through the flock so that each bird has to give way to a more dominant bird, but can get his way over less aggressive birds. The order of positions within a group of birds is called the *peck order*. Each bird recognizes its position and accepts it, and does not have to fight to keep it. In this way, squabbling within the flock is prevented. Being at the bottom end of a peck order is not always pleasant; when food is scarce, these timid birds have no chance of eating. They stand a better chance of surviving by leaving the flock and hunting for food on their own.

Birds of different species may get together to seek food, and a peck order will come into being in a mixed group as well as a flock of the same birds.

BEHAVING ALIKE

If you observe a flock of birds, you will see that most of the birds are behaving in the same way at the same time, whether they are bathing, resting, feeding or preening. If one bird starts to bathe, then its action often makes the others join in until most of the flock is bathing. Humans often behave in a similar way. Someone laughing heartily, or yawning, often makes others react in the same way.

THE LANGUAGE OF BIRDS

Birds "talk" to each other, just as we do. They can make clear to other birds just who they are or what they are doing or what they want to do. Like us, they use sound signals and visual signals that others can hear or see. But the ways in which birds use such signals are very different from the ways we use them.

We depend more on our faces to indicate our moods and less on gestures and postures of our bodies. A smile or a frown can mean a lot, and a movement of the wrist or a position of the body usually only serves to emphasize a point we are making in some other way. Birds are very different. The expression on a bird's face hardly ever changes, although opening the beak may indicate something. But ruffling up the feathers, spreading the wings or adopting certain body postures mean very special things to birds, and are very important to them.

Below: Many birds have striking markings that enable other birds of the same species to recognize them. In the Willet (1), Oystercatcher (2) and American Avocet (3), these markings show during flight, but are hidden when the birds are on the ground or in the water.

These actions can show anger or fear, and whether the bird is going to attack or fly away. They make a precise language clearly understood by other birds.

BIRD MARKINGS

Every species of bird has its own special markings. These markings identify the bird, just as the symbols painted on the body and wings of an aircraft show to which airline or country it belongs. Birds that live in flocks will see another bird with the same markings and fly towards it. But solitary birds that like to be alone will fly away as soon as they see a fellow bird.

Markings that stand out may attract enemies as well as fellow birds, especially when birds live together in flocks. So many social birds have markings on the tail, rump or wings that are hidden until they spread their wings. On the ground, they are inconspicuous and are therefore less vulnerable prey.

Above: The songs of the Nightingale, Nightjar and Savi's Warbler (top to bottom) are loud and continue without stopping. Although one might think such a noise would attract enemies, these birds are well camouflaged by their plumage and may sing at night under cover of darkness.

Above: The Blackbird (left) has a musical song but sings close to cover so that it cannot be seen. The Ring Ouzel, which lives in open moorland and is more easily spotted, has a song that does not easily give away its position.

Left: A male chaffinch sings to defend its territory. The song informs other birds that the singer is a chaffinch, is male, is holding some territory it has gained, and that it is singing from its territory and defying others to try and take its territory away. Young chaffinches have a basic inborn ability to sing, but they learn to sing correctly from other chaffinches. If a young bird is kept from hearing others of its kind, it will develop a song which lasts the right length of time and has the proper notes but is not phrased correctly. This will prevent it from being able to communicate properly.

But the signals can be seen as soon as the birds take flight, and help to keep the flock together.

Different kinds of birds that fly and feed together may even have similar markings to help keep them in a group and ensure their survival.

CALLING AND SINGING

Making sounds is as important to birds as it is to people. Every bird has a repertoire of sound signals for different purposes. The Great Tit has as many as 40 different cries, but most birds make do with from one dozen to two dozen. There are two general kinds of cries: *call notes* and *song*.

Call notes can mean many things. One call may mean "Here I am, where are you?" and may be used by birds in a flock to keep together. Special flight calls get birds into a flying mood, and both kinds of call notes are especially useful to birds that migrate by night. Calls can also mean danger, and danger signals are also often similar among different birds. The kind of call depends on the kind of enemy that is approaching. A perched bird of prey, a fox or a cat will receive a *mobbing* call. This kind of call is easy to locate and lets all the birds round about know where the enemy is. Mobbing calls sound like "chinks" or "chacks", and the responding birds will gather to attack, or mob, their enemy. Birds of prey on the

Above: A pair of Australian Gannets preen each other. This action is a way of saying "keep calm", and prevents aggression.

Above: Some Oystercatchers pipe together for the same reason.

Left: The aggressive display (1) and the appeasement display (2) of the European Jay are very different. In the appeasement display, the bird points its bill up to show that it is ready to withdraw. The Sandwich Tern points its bill at a rival bird to threaten it (3). To appease a rival, the bird's weapon is pointed away (4).

Below: A male Crimson Finch and a female Zebra Finch communicate by postures. The Zebra Finch accidentally lands too close to the Crimson Finch (top), who stretches out his body in a horizontal posture of aggression. The Zebra Finch stands upright (centre), on the defensive, and finally flies away (bottom).

wing, however, get a danger call like a high-pitched "see-e-e". This call is not easy to locate, as the caller does not want to give away its position, but it serves to warn the other birds to flee for cover.

Song is a form of language that birds use during the breeding season. A song may attract a female to a male and put her in the right mood for mating. But the song of the male may also be a warning to other males to keep away. Birds that are otherwise much alike may have very different songs so that a female is not attracted to the wrong kind of male. The song itself may also be designed for survival. Birds that live in open country do not advertise their presence to enemies with songs that can be easily located. Birds that cannot be seen easily, on the other hand, may sing loudly and continuously, unafraid of being spotted.

PEACE TALKS

Living together in groups, as most birds prefer to live, often presents problems. But, sensibly, birds mostly avoid fighting and will settle a dispute by exchanging signals to indicate that one bird will back down and withdraw. The aggressive bird adopts a *display* – a posture or a gesture – showing his hostility. The peace-making bird adopts an appeasement display, and so prevents combat.

SETTING ABOUT BREEDING

Breeding is essential for every animal. If the animals of one particular species do not produce enough young to make up for the number of their kind that die, then these animals will gradually decrease in number and eventually become extinct. This has happened, even quite recently. In the 1800s, there were millions of Passenger Pigeons in America. Then men killed so many for eating that the pigeons could not breed fast enough to survive. By 1914, they had become extinct.

Birds usually breed at a certain time of the year, called the *breeding season*. The birds come together, and each male selects a territory in which to breed. The male must attract a female mate and the pair must build a nest, hatch the eggs, feed their young and protect them from enemies. For most birds, this kind of co-operation demands a temporary change of behaviour patterns.

The changes in behaviour are produced by the release of certain chemicals called *hormones* in the bird's body. Hormones influence human behaviour too. In birds they bring about a whole language of courtship. The birds exchange signals in order to seize territories and attract their mates, and to reduce the mutual feeling of fear that a pair of birds would normally have. Only then can the birds mate, lay their eggs and rear their young.

Above: Yellow-eyed Penguins of New Zealand form couples or pairs that stay together for many years. Observers kept watch on one pair that bred each year for thirteen years. The male is on the left, the female on the right.

Left: The male Ring-necked Pheasant is a brightly-coloured bird. It takes no part in rearing its young because its plumage would attract enemies to the nest. The females in the background are dull-coloured and less easily seen, and they rear the young.

Most birds split up into pairs to breed. Some pairs breed together year after year, just as many humans form marriage partnerships to have their children. But some birds breed in groups rather than pairs and others may have more than one mate. In some species, such as the Painted Snipe, the female may mate with several males. Once the eggs have been laid, the males take over hatching them and rearing the young.

DEFENDING A TERRITORY

Most birds breed in territories which they often fight to obtain. Each pair of birds has its own breeding territory and no other birds of the same species are allowed to enter. Small perching birds may command a territory of less than a hectare (two acres). But the Golden Eagle is master of a vast territory as large as 75 square km. The male fights to keep its territory intact. The robin that we find so friendly is by no means so benevolent to other robins. In spring, robins show off their red breasts as a threat to other robins. If a red breast should be sighted, it is savagely assaulted. This can happen even if the visitor is not another robin but a chaffinch with a pinky-red breast. Even a bunch of red feathers placed inside a robin's territory will fool it into attacking.

Below: The Great Bustard attracts a mate by advertising itself. Normally the male is a drab brownish bird, but when it wants to find a female, it suddenly displays magnificent white plumage. The Great Bustard lives in Europe and Asia. It may stand a metre tall and is one of the largest flying birds. Great Bustards are rare birds and live under protection.

Right: The Black Grouse attracts its mate by adopting a strange posture and crowing and singing in a bubbling but musical way. The Black Grouse lives in forests in Europe and Asia. The males have special display grounds, called *leks*, where many gather and perform their odd antics to attract the females. Each male has its own territory.

The birds are especially keen on keeping their territories because they are refuges for courting and mating. They may also contain the birds' food supply. But many birds' territories are larger than they need to feed themselves. The defended areas become smaller when the bird population in a region increases, but this does not seem to affect breeding.

Birds do not always feed in their own territories. Oystercatchers have two territories. One is inland where the birds rear their young, and the other is on the shore where the adults feed. The parents commute between the two territories to bring food to the young. Many sea birds use their small nesting areas for courting and rearing chicks. But the birds fly far and wide in search of food and do not have feeding territories.

Although fighting over territories makes pairs of birds space themselves out to breed, the territories often join one another so that they form neighbourhoods of breeding birds. Not all birds have large individual territories. Black-headed gulls nest in colonies where the nests are about a metre apart. Nesting too closely gives enemies such as Carrion Crows a better chance of finding the eggs. But if the nests are too far apart, the gulls will not come to each other's aid if they should be attacked.

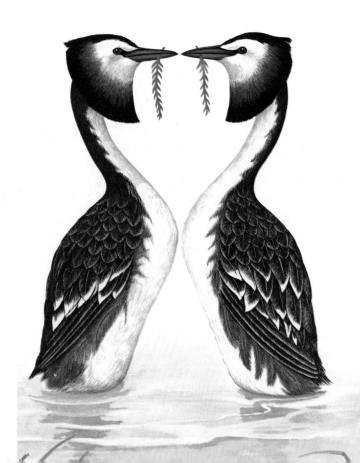

Left: Great Crested Grebes have several kinds of displays for courtship. The "penguin" dance is a lively intricate dance in which both birds rush together, rear up face to face, and dive to bring up pieces of weed in their beaks.

Opposite page: Crowned Cranes have a wild courtship dance, in which they leap and prance. These cranes live in Africa and migrate north for the summer. When the cranes arrive at their summer home, they split up into pairs and the dances commence. The male moves towards the female, bowing with his neck bent forward. Then he leaps into the air several times, making trumpeting calls. His mate joins in, splashing about in the shallow water where the dances take place.

Above and opposite page: North Atlantic Gannets have several courtship displays. Bowing (1 and 2) is done by the male bird to draw a female's attention to a nest site. It consists of head shaking followed by bowing, and keeps away other males. Male advertising (3) brings the females to the nest site. It is a less aggressive posture. Facing away (4) is the female's gesture as she intrudes into the male's territory. The female hides her bill, a peaceful gesture, to win the male's confidence. Mutual fencing (5 and 6) involves dipping, mainly by the male, and crossing the bills like scissors. This helps the gannets by reducing any fear or aggression they may have. Sky pointing (7 and 8) is a signal given when one bird is about to leave. It is a sign to the other bird to stay, so that the nest is not left unguarded.

Left: Many displays that birds perform come from the first part of the take-off leap. A Mallard Duck adopts a posture with its head up and tail up (1). This is one of many gestures that make up the courtship ritual of the Mallard. A Mute Swan threatens a rival (2). A Cormorant flaps its wings rhythmically to show off the white patches on its thighs (3). The courtship posture of the Hooded Merganser involves putting its head back (4). All these postures are derived from the first part of the take-off leap.

Above: A diagram of a bird about to take off. It coils itself up like a spring before leaping into the air.

ATTRACTING A MATE

Once a bird is on its territory and so has a nesting site, it must lure a mate there to breed. There is great competition for good sites, and a bird cannot rest if he is to keep his site. It has to advertise its presence to other males to keep them away as well as to female birds to make them approach.

Birds can use song to do this, and birds that live among trees and bushes or under cover of darkness will sing loudly and continuously to proclaim their territories and call for mates. The song also serves to

Right: Birds perform several courtship displays that are similar to the second part of the take-off leap. The Goldeneye has a display in which it stretches out its body in the water (1). The Great Crested Grebe has a threatening display that consists of stretching its body forward (2). This display is given to a rival bird. The displays of this Heron also have a stretch phase (3). The Hooded Merganser also assumes a stretching posture as part of its courtship (4). This bird therefore has postures that come from both the first and second parts of the take-off leap. The posture that comes from the first part is shown on the opposite page.

Above: A diagram of a bird making the second part of its take-off leap. After coiling up like a spring, the bird straightens out, arrow-like, as it leaps into the air. The final position resembles the final position of a clean dive into a swimming pool.

tell the female where the male is located. The foghorn call of the Bittern, for example, booms out over the reed beds like a beacon of sound. Every day during the breeding season, birds re-establish their territories at dawn and sunset with a boisterous chorus of song.

Song is not the only language that a bird can use to court its mate: it may have special plumage and adopt unusual postures to lure a female. Many birds use both sound and visual language in courtship. But some may rely entirely on their strange appearance at breeding time to get a mate.

Below: Like the Shelduck, the male Mandarin Duck has a courtship ritual that is similar to preening. But the Mandarin Duck just touches its sail-like wing feather with its bill, instead of burying its bill in its rump feathers.

Above: The courtship gestures of some ducks are similar to the movements they make when preening. The bird bends its head as if to take some oil from its oil gland. In courting, this is a nervous gesture, performed when the male is feeling unsure about the response of the female.

COURTSHIP CEREMONIES

Any gentleman knows that he must behave in a certain well-mannered way to appeal to a lady, although exactly what he must do depends very much on the particular society in which he lives. Birds also have all sorts of ceremonies to accompany courtship. A pair of birds establishes a bond by exchanging signals which reduce the fear and aggression between them. This bond then has to be kept up by more ceremonies.

Right: Two Herring Gulls face away from each other. This is a movement that reduces aggression between the birds. Herring Gulls are aggressive birds and their aggression must be quelled if the birds are ever to get together to breed. Facing away happens early in the courtship, when the two birds are not completely used to each other. Turning the head away like this hides the bill from the partner, and is an important peacemaking ceremony.

Opposite page A Herring Gull tears up some tussocks of grass. This bird has been confronted by another male in a dispute about territory. It does not want to attack the other bird, and so furiously rips up the grass instead. This is ritual behaviour and serves to warn the opponent, "This could happen to you, so leave me alone."

Some of the most beautiful courtship ceremonies are performed by the Great Crested Grebe. In the "cat" display, a courting bird adopts a cat-like defensive posture. In the "penguin" dance, the two birds rush towards each other, rear up breast to breast, and dive to pick up pieces of weed in their beaks! (See page 38.) Two mated birds may also perform a head shaking ceremony. Such ceremonies have grown out of other types of bird behaviour and have evolved into rituals with special meanings.

Exaggerated movements and postures make the ceremonies highly distinctive, and birds may have special markings to increase the impact on their mates. The way a peacock displays itself during the breeding season is something that even humans find unforgettable.

Rituals may come from several kinds of behaviour. Stylized versions of movements normally used while drinking or preening can become parts of courtship ceremonies. The way a bird takes off on a flight gives rise to many kinds of displays (see pages 40 and 41).

In some birds, a whole series of take-off leaps have evolved into courtship dances. Male Gouldian Finches of Australia perform a jumping dance in front of the female finches. By ruffling up their plumage to frame their heads in cobalt blue, and enlarging their lilac breast patches, they look most spectacular. The male Zebra Finch does a dance in which it hops towards the female and then turns away, swinging its body all the time. This shows the conflict between approaching and avoiding another bird that makes up many rituals.

Above: Birds perform many gestures during their courtship that may seem to have nothing to do with the courtship itself. The Spice Finch (top) has a special posture called the *low twist*, which is a beak wipe that never actually gets performed. The bird stops before the beak rubs against the perch. The Madagascar Lovebird (bottom) often scratches its head. This is normal be-haviour in lovebirds which, contrary to their name, are often very hostile to their mates. But the Black-masked Lovebird (centre) scratches as a courtship gesture. It raises its foot to its red bill, possibly to draw attention to its brightly-coloured plumage.

Left: A male Red Avadavat goes through a courtship ritual that is similar to its nest-building movements. It takes a piece of twig in its beak as it bows to the female. This display comes from the movements that the avadavat makes as it tucks in twigs to build its nest. These pretty little birds live in Asia and their strange name is a corruption of Ahmadabad, the Indian city from where the first avadavats were sent to Europe. They live in flocks in marsh land and wet grassland. Red Avadavats make tame cage birds.

Some activities of courtship appear to have nothing to do with the purpose of breeding. A bird may suddenly scratch, wipe its beak or preen its feathers, like the ducks shown on page 42. These movements actually help to relieve the bird's anxiety when it is in a situation of conflict and feels nervous. They are called *displacement activities*. People have such activities. Scratching the head, tapping the feet, and even smoking a cigarette are activities that often help us to get through a difficult situation. Many other displays in bird courtship are intended to calm the mate so as to keep the bond between the two birds intact.

If a bird's courtship is successful, it is soon followed by the building of a nest. It is not surprising then to find that some courtship rituals resemble nest building. The "penguin" dance of the

Left: An Adélie Penguin offers its mate a pebble. Stones are valuable objects to possess in the snowy wastes of Antarctica where these penguins live, as nothing else is available to build nests. Gathering pebbles is the part of the nest-building routine which has also become part of the birds' courtship behaviour. The pebbles are often stolen from the nest pile of a neighbouring penguin! Adélie Penguins return to the same colony to breed every year, and they build their nests of pebbles on almost the same spot every time.

Left: The Peacock (top) and the male Argus Pheasant perform two of the most spectacular bird displays. They erect great fans of feathers. The Peacock uses its upper tail coverts (covering feathers) and the Argus Pheasant uses its wing feathers, which makes it difficult for it to fly. The Peacock's feathers are beautifully adorned with eye-spots of iridescent colours, and are as much admired by humans as by the Peahen!

Great Crested Grebes, in which the birds pick up pieces of weed, is an example. Herons, too, pass nest material to each other during courtship.

SHOWING OFF

It is not always easy for us to hide our feelings. Feeling embarrassed can make us blush scarlet and anger can even make us shake with rage. Ashamed as we may feel of these reactions, we can do little to stop them.

Birds act in similar ways, although not for the same reasons. Turkeys blush to attract a mate. Many kinds of courtship displays consist of ruffling the feathers in various ways. Several birds, including turkeys, raise the feathers all over their bodies as they strut before their mates. Other birds ruffle only certain parts of their plumage. These parts may have markings that stand out when they are ruffled. Sometimes, raising the feathers may reveal hidden markings underneath that attract a mate.

Some birds have displays of feathers that are very striking to see. They show off beautiful crests, beards, tufts, plumes and trains of feathers in displays during courtship. The direction in which the bird presents itself to its mate depends on which region of its body the bird uses in such a display. The beautiful Golden Pheasant presents itself sideways on,

Below: Large birds such as turkeys may blush red when they want to attract their mates. The blue skin on a male turkey's head and neck turns scarlet. But, unlike people, a turkey does not feel embarrassed when he blushes. He is just showing his interest in the female turkey. Turkeys also fluff up their feathers as they posture before their mates.

because it has a superb cape of golden plumage around its neck that is best seen from the side. The Peacock erects a magnificent fan of iridescent feathers to frame its bright blue head and neck. This is an irresistible sight to the Peahen when it sees the Peacock from the front.

People often "display" to each other rather like birds do, particularly in the way they arrange their hair and wear their clothes. We talk of someone being "as proud as a peacock".

ACTING LIKE A BABY AGAIN

Some courtship rituals are very strange and involve one bird behaving as if it were a baby bird. Usually the female begs food from the male in the same way that the young birds in the nest get food from their parents. Male Red Avadavats use the same wing movement when forming pairs with females as they did when they wanted to be fed while still very young. It is possible that seeing one bird "acting young" makes the other bird feel like a parent, and so stops any fear or aggression that it might be feeling towards its partner.

Above: Many male birds have special feathers they use to attract the attention of the female. The male Capercaillie (top) has a beard, just as many men grow a beard in an endeavour to attract women. Leadbeater's Cockatoo of Australia (centre) raises a superb crest of red and pink feathers as part of its courtship. The Bluecrowned Pigeon of New Guinea (bottom) wears a permanent crown of lacy blue feathers. It is a huge pigeon, nearly a metre in length.

Left: Two young Red Avadavats beg food from an adult female bird (top). They do this by raising one wing. When the adults wish to form a pair for breeding, the male raises its wing in a similar way to attract the female (bottom).

Opposite page: A male Goldfinch stands over a female and offers her food as she sits on the nest. This is courtship behaviour, which takes place before mating, and it comes from the behaviour of young birds. Courtship feeding is a ritual followed by many birds. Usually the female sits on a nest and begs her food from the male, just as she begged food from her parents when she was young. This kind of behaviour helps to keep the birds together. If the female sits on the eggs all the time, "free" feeding like this is essential. Hornbills build their nests around the female, who has to be fed in this way.

HOLDING COURT

Most birds form pairs that stay together for the breeding season. But some birds only come together to mate for a few short moments during the season, and they otherwise live apart.

This brief union is achieved in a strange way. The males gather together on special display grounds called *arenas* or *leks*. Each bird in the lek defends a small plot of its own called a *court*. The size of the lek varies. The Greater Prairie Chicken, a grouse that lives in North America, carries out its displays in arenas up to 200 m wide and 800 m long. An arena this size holds about 400 male birds. Most male "lek" birds have splendid plumage that they show off in their courts to attract the females. When the females arrive, they take their choice of the males on display. They may fly from lek to lek before finally retiring to lay their eggs.

Ruffs are unusual lek birds that live in Europe and Asia. They get their name from the large collars or ruffs of coloured feathers around their heads and necks. The ruffs vary in colour from black, through brown, red or yellow to white. None of the males is exactly alike, and telling one from another is easy.

The males also behave differently. Some males are *resident* males who hold their own courts. They are aggressive birds with dark coloured ruffs. There are also *satellite* males that do not possess their own courts, but they associate with resident males. The satellite males usually have white ruffs and are less aggressive than the resident males. On a large lek, only the resident males mate. But on smaller leks, the presence of the satellite males increases the chances of mating for both resident males and satellite males.

Some lek birds have magnificent plumage to attract the females. One of these is the bright red male Cock-of-the-Rock. The female has the same plumage, but is brown. The Superb Lyre Bird is a spectacular arena bird. Each male clears up to ten courts in the undergrowth, into which the females are enticed. As the male proceeds with the display, it brings its ornate silvery tail over its head like a "fairy parasol". A lyre bird adopting this pose is a sight of rare and moving beauty.

Birds of paradise, which come from New Guinea and northern Australia, are some of the most ornamental birds in the world. At least 24 of these birds display in arenas. The bird of paradise attracts its mate by a fantastic display of plumes. The 43 species have an amazing variety of adornments – strange long plumes that fall like ribbons from the tail or head and sprays of lacy feathers that form beautiful mists of colour. The display behaviour of the bird of paradise shows its beauty to full effect. The Magnificent Bird of Paradise is so "vain" about its appearance that it pulls away leaves from the undergrowth around its court so that more light can fall on to its glistening plumage.

But birds of paradise are not the only birds that go to such lengths to charm their mates. The other great wooers of the bird world are related to the birds of paradise and live in the same part of the globe. These are the amazing bower birds.

Below: The male Satin Bower Bird builds an avenue along which the female, shown behind, must be enticed before mating takes place. The avenues are extremely intricate. The male bird first clears a space in the undergrowth, and covers the space with a mat of sticks and twigs. Then it builds two parallel fences of upright sticks. These sticks are stuck firmly in the ground and entwined together, sometimes bending over to meet overhead. The fences are far enough apart for the female to walk into the avenue. The floor is decorated with blue objects such as flowers and feathers. The inside of the walls of the avenue is daubed with a blue or green "paint" made by mixing charcoal and other pigments with saliva. The bower bird, one of a few species which can use a tool, applies the paint by holding a wad of bark in its beak. After mating, the female leaves the avenue to build a nest, and hatches and rears the young on her own. Outside the breeding season, these bower birds travel about eastern Australia in small flocks of 4 to 6 birds. They live on berries and fruits, as well as insects.

BLOSSOMS, BIRDS AND BOWERS

Bower birds are not as spectacular to look at as the birds of paradise. A few males of the 19 species have special head plumes and bright colours, but most are fairly dull in appearance. They make up for this by building special bowers of twigs and sticks and then decorating the bowers with flowers and plants, and even painting them. The skill of the bower bird as an architect and decorator is matched nowhere else in the whole animal world.

But, skilled builder though it is, the male bower bird does not use its ability to build a nest. Its carefully constructed bower is intended only for mating purposes. The female bower bird is lured into the bower and mating takes place. After her visit, she goes off alone to build a nest, lay her eggs, and bring up the young.

Above: The stage-maker bower birds are the simplest of the bower birds. They clear courts in the undergrowth and decorate them with fresh leaves from certain kinds of trees. The Tooth-billed Bower Bird cuts the leaves off the trees with the saw-like notches along its bill and places them with the pale sides uppermost on the ground. If the leaves are turned over, the male bower bird will replace them with the pale side up. As the leaves wither, the bird gets fresh ones and the court becomes surrounded by a circle of dead leaves. The bird spends much time singing and calling from a perch above his court, trying to attract a female. It is a good mimic.

Left: The birds of paradise from the New Guinea region are among the most ornamental birds in the world. These three birds of paradise are the Magnificent Riflebird (1), the King of Saxony's Bird of Paradise (2), and the Magnificent Bird of Paradise (3). They are birds that display in arenas, and are shown here in display postures. The Magnificent Bird of Paradise makes its display even more astonishing by trimming away the leaves around its court so that more light can reach its glistening plumage.

Right: The Crestless Gardener is a bower bird of western New Guinea. It displays on a court to attract the female bower bird to mate, and entices her there by building a magnificent bower about 1m high. This bower bird is one of several bower birds called maypole builders. It begins its task by piling up a pyramid of twigs and sticks around the foot of a small tree. It then builds a tent-like hut over the pyramid and constructs a low stockade to mark out a "garden" in front of its hut. The bower bird then decorates the floor of its bower, the pyramid inside and the garden with flowers and other plants, berries and snail shells. The bird even replaces dying flowers with fresh ones! The female is enticed into this enchanting "love nest" to mate, after which she leaves to lay her eggs and bring up the young. These bower birds may return to their bowers year after year and repair and extend them. Large bowers may take several years to complete.

Two of the 19 species of bower birds do not construct bowers. The three varieties of *stage-maker* bower birds make the simplest bowers by clearing a "stage" in the undergrowth 1 m to 2 m across, rather like a miniature circus ring. The bird adorns the stage with leaves, and one stage-maker even erects a curtain of bamboo and ferns around its stage.

Five of the bower birds are called *maypole builders*, because their bowers are built around tree trunks just as maypole dancers construct a fan of ribbons around a pole. Some of the maypole builders are called gardeners because they plant mosses in and around their bowers, and decorate their courts with ferns and blossoms, replacing them with fresh plants as they wilt. The bowers may be repaired and extended every year, and can reach a height of 3 m!

The remaining 9 species of bower birds are called *avenue builders*. They construct walled avenues of twigs and sticks; two of these birds actually daub the walls with a paint of saliva and pigments! They pick up wads of leaves or bark to use as brushes, and are among the very few kinds of birds that use tools.

NESTING AND LOOKING AFTER THE YOUNG

After their courtship and mating, birds have to build nests to house first the eggs, and then the infant birds until they are old enough to look after themselves. Sometimes the males and females work together in gathering material and weaving it into a nest. Kingfishers work in pairs to excavate a tunnel in the river bank, and then scoop out a nesting chamber at the end of the tunnel. But many birds are less co-operative. The males have to do most of the work when weaverbirds and grassfinches decide to nest. In the manakins, vireos, hummingbirds and finches, the female is the home maker.

But whoever does it, nest building is hard work. Barn Swallows make nests shaped like flasks and plastered with mud, often in the rafters of barns or sheds. Bird watchers have observed that a pair of swallows makes more than 1,200 trips to carry enough mud to the nest site. All this effort demands a lot of energy, and must be timed so that the nest is finished when the eggs are laid. It is not by coincidence that birds get their nests built on time. Their feverish activity is triggered off by certain events.

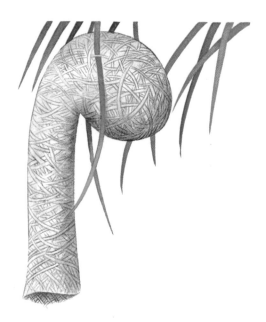

Above: Some weaver birds build intricate nests with entrance tunnels hanging down below a nesting chamber.

Below left: The female canary starts to build a nest as the days get longer and courtship begins (1). Her brood patch then becomes sensitive (2). This causes her to line the nest with soft feathers (3).

Above: Social Weavers of South Africa work together, as many as 600 at a time, to build huge communal nests in trees.

Right: A Tailor Bird of eastern Asia stitches its home together like a tailor using a needle and thread. The bird makes holes in the edges of some large green leaves, knots fibres of cotton or other plant fibres and threads the ends through the holes with its beak. Then it pulls the threads to draw the leaves together to fashion a cup, which it lines with soft materials to make a nest.

Female canaries build their nests in two parts. First they make a cup of rough grass and twigs and then they line the cup with soft feathers to make it comfortable. The female bird starts to feel the need to build a nest when a chemical called *oestrogen*, which is a female sex hormone, builds up in her body. This happens when the number of hours of daylight increases day by day – that is, in the spring. In addition, the courtship of the male canary intensifies at this time and helps to produce more oestrogen. The female starts on the nest. As she does so, the build-up of oestrogen makes her shed some feathers from her breast, leaving bare, sensitive brood patches. Because the grass and twigs will scratch the sensitive brood patches if she tries to sit on the nest, the canary finishes it off by lining it with feathers. The soft feathers keep her comfortable and, with the mother bird's warm brood patches, surround the eggs as she sits on them.

NESTS, NESTS, NESTS

There are almost as many different types of nests as there are different types of birds. Some birds do not build any nests at all. King Penguins and Emperor Penguins lay single eggs which the males hold on their feet and under folds of skin on their bellies. The penguins are thus able to keep their eggs warm in the icy lands where they live. At the other end of the nest-building scale are the Social Weavers. They live in

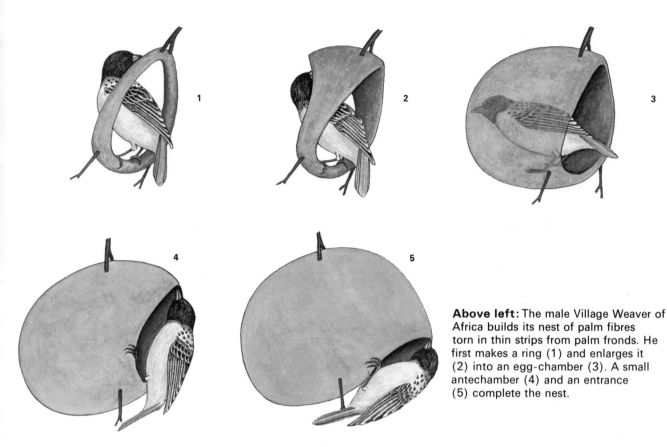

Above left: The male Village Weaver of Africa builds its nest of palm fibres torn in thin strips from palm fronds. He first makes a ring (1) and enlarges it (2) into an egg-chamber (3). A small antechamber (4) and an entrance (5) complete the nest.

communities, where as many as 300 pairs of birds may build a vast nest to house an entire colony. These "apartment blocks" cover whole trees. Other great nest builders are the megapodes of Australasia. These birds bury their eggs in great mounds of rotting plants, which provide the heat to keep the eggs warm. The largest mounds reach a height of about 3 m, and are as much as 16 m across!

The shape of a nest may depend on how safe the nest site is from enemies. Guillemots live on ledges on cliffs, and are secure there. They do not build nests, and the eggs are pear-shaped so that they spin round on the spot instead of rolling over the cliff. Some perching birds of the tropics build nests with long entrance tunnels, like socks hanging upside-down from a washing line, which prevent snakes and other enemies getting into the nests and stealing the eggs.

Birds use all sorts of materials to make nests. Some swiftlets make their nests almost entirely of their own saliva. It may take a swiftlet as long as 40 days to construct its nest. Some swallows use mud; the Eider Duck uses fibres, stones, and feathers; some penguins make nests only of pebbles; and Crested Flycatchers even use snake skins!

INCUBATING THE EGGS

Each of the eggs produced by a mated female bird contains a live embryo bird. The eggs we eat at the table come from unmated female chickens, and do not contain embryos. The embryo must be kept warm inside the egg, or it will die. It lives on the yolk and grows until it occupies the complete interior of the shell. Then it is ready to hatch. The time that the embryo spends inside the egg is called the *incubation period*. This period is only 10 days for small perching birds. The Royal Albatross has the longest known incubation period – 80 days.

Most birds have brood patches which fit over the eggs and keep them warm. Gannets and cormorants have especially warm feet with which to incubate the eggs. Female birds usually have the task of incubating. Male Hornbills make sure it gets done by sealing the female into the nest together with the eggs! A small hole is left open in the nest so that the male can feed the female. Male birds that are brightly coloured must not spend much time near the nest for fear of attracting enemies. The incubating is best left to their more camouflaged mates. However, in more than half the families of birds, both males and females share the incubation.

Not all birds use their own body heat to incubate the eggs. The megapodes of Australasia bury their eggs in mounds of rotting plants like giant compost heaps. The eggs must be kept at 33°C, whatever the weather outside the mound. To keep the temperature the same, the male bird has to work for up to 13 hours every day. He scrapes material from the top of the mound if it gets too hot inside (it may reach 45°C)

Above: The Mallee Fowl of Australia buries its eggs under a mound of rotting plants. This material keeps the eggs warm and the Mallee Fowl does not have to sit on its eggs to hatch them. The bird instinctively knows that it must pile on more plants at night, when it is cold, to keep the eggs warm (right), and scrape some away in the morning (left) when the air is warmer.

Below: A female Whitethroat sitting on her nest shows no concern for an egg that has dropped out of the nest. Several other birds behave in this way towards eggs which become displaced from the nest. These birds are not stupid and heartless, but seem to know that trying to get the egg back into the nest makes little sense, because it is almost certainly broken.

Above: The King Penguin does not build a nest. It keeps its egg warm by holding the egg on its feet and enveloping it in a fold of skin. The Emperor Penguin incubates its egg in the same way. These birds are the largest penguins and only have one egg. Nesting materials are hard to find in the icy southern wastes where they live, and so they have found a way of doing without a nest. The embryo penguin develops inside the egg as long as it is kept warm. But if the egg is exposed even for a moment to the freezing temperatures, the embryo dies. The incubation period lasts for more than 60 days, and the male penguin guards the egg for all this time without eating. During incubation, the female is away feeding. As soon as the young penguin hatches out, the female returns to take charge and the male goes off to eat.

Right: The Common Cuckoo is one of several birds that lay their eggs in the nests of other birds.

so as to allow heat to escape. In the evening, he must build up the mound to prevent the cool night air making the eggs inside the mound too cold.

In this way, the male stops the eggs being chilled or cooked. To do so, he must know what the temperature is inside the mound. The megapode does this by taking samples of soil or compost from the mound and pressing the sample against his heat-sensitive palate or tongue. Incubation is a long business, for it lasts up to 8 or 9 weeks. When the baby megapodes eventually hatch, they wriggle their way up through the mounds to the air. The hatchlings already have feathers and are even able to fly, so the parent bird has no more work to do after its exhausting vigil.

Other birds behave in a similar way to the megapodes. The Mallee Fowl of Australia bury their eggs in mounds. Zoologists studied this fowl by placing an electric heating element inside its mound. They found that the fowl scraped away soil from the mound as soon as the heater was switched on. In this way, they proved that the male bird was responding to the temperature inside the mound and not to any other factor.

The Maleo Fowl of the Celebes islands in Indonesia lays its eggs one by one in the black volcanic sand found along the beaches there. The sand absorbs the heat of the sun and the eggs incubate with no further help. This bird may also bury its eggs near active volcanoes where the soil is warmed by steam – just like central heating!

Above: A young cuckoo.

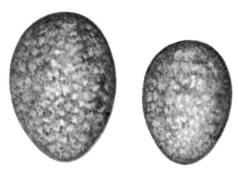

Above: A cuckoo egg (left) and the egg of its foster parent, a Reed Warbler (right), look very much alike.

STRANGERS IN THE NEST

Some birds do not make nests and do not bring up young. They survive by laying their eggs in the nests of other birds and letting these foster parents rear their young for them. These brood parasites, as they are called, include Black-headed Ducks, honey-guides, cow birds, weaver birds, viduine weavers, and 47 kinds of cuckoos.

The parasite birds are usually very particular about which host birds are suitable to bring up their young. The eggs of both birds must be about the same size and colour, and both must have about the same incubation period. The young intruder must receive the right food, but it has to make the right kind of signals to its foster parent in order to be fed and stop the parent feeding its own young instead.

The European Cuckoo is a well-known brood parasite. It lays its eggs in the nests of more than 120 other species of birds. But each female cuckoo probably only uses one kind of host bird. It lays only one egg in the host's nest, and removes one of the eggs already in the nest to fool the foster parent. A cuckoo that lays brown eggs will place its egg in the nest of a meadow pipit, which also lays brown eggs. Cuckoos that have bluish eggs will lay them in the nests of hedge sparrows, where they mingle with the sparrow's own blue eggs.

Once the young cuckoo hatches, it takes over. The other young birds are ruthlessly heaved out of the

Left: These male Paradise Whydahs (left) make elaborate courtship postures. The birds live in Africa, and lay their eggs in the nests of Melba Finches (above). But they only use the varieties of finches that live in the southern and eastern parts of their range. The female lays two or three eggs in the host's nest. Unlike cuckoos, the young whydahs do not push their foster brothers and sisters out of the nest.

Left: The male Pin-tailed Whydah calls the attention of the female to a male Violet-eared Waxbill that is building a nest. Whydahs lay their eggs in the nests of waxbills, and the parent waxbills rear the young whydahs. The relationship between the two different birds is very close. The female whydah does not feel like breeding until she sees the male waxbill preparing to breed. The call that the male whydah uses to attract her attention to the waxbill is very similar to the nest call of the waxbill itself. The female whydahs in fact prefer to mate with male whydahs that can imitate waxbills in this way!

nest and thus cannot compete with the intruder for food. The young cuckoo has a huge yellow mouth with great fleshy flanges on both sides. The sight of this gaping mouth spurs the foster parents into bringing food. Such is its appetite that one intruding cuckoo can eat enough to make up for the whole brood that it replaces.

The European Cuckoo and other cuckoos of the Old World are the best known of parasite birds. Among them, they use more than 300 other species of birds to bring up their young. In North and South America, most of the cuckoos do not behave in such a way. The Yellow-billed Cuckoo and the Black-billed Cuckoo sometimes lay eggs in other nests, but the main parasite birds in the New World are cow birds. The honeyguides of Africa are savagely effective as parasites. The young honeyguides are born with sharp hooks on their bills. They use these hooks to kill the other birds in the nest, usually baby woodpeckers. The hooks drop off as soon as this grisly work is done. Honeyguide eggs are laid one to a nest. If more than one honeyguide were born in a nest, one would kill the other.

This behaviour may seem dreadful to us, but both parasite birds and host birds are behaving instinctively – it is the only way they know how to behave.

Below: A Black-headed Gull removes pieces of egg shell from its nest. This action helps the gull and its young to survive. The inside of the egg is white, and any pieces of egg shell lying about will stand out. If the shells were not removed, enemies such as Carrion Crows (below left) would see the white fragments gleaming against the dark nest, and would attack the newly-hatched birds. Therefore, the parent gull carries the egg shells to a safe distance from the nest shortly after the young hatch out. Not all gulls behave in the same prudent way as the Black-headed Gull. Herring Gulls are large, ferocious birds and can take care of such enemies, so they need not worry about hiding their nests. Kittiwakes nest on sheer cliff faces, where they are rarely bothered by Carrion Crows.

BODYGUARDS

Like human parents, birds are always concerned with keeping their young out of danger. The position of the nest and the way it is disguised by camouflage help to avoid the attentions of enemies. But some birds need help to protect their young.

Several species of birds, such as auks, gulls and herons, nest with their own kind in great colonies. These birds find safety in numbers. Other birds team up with aggressive animals, which act rather like bodyguards. In South America, small tanagers and Tyrant Flycatchers will nest near aggressive birds like the Kiskadee, which has no fear of raiders. Red-tailed Buzzards, Marabou Storks, Snowy Owls and Pied Crows often have more defenceless birds nesting near their own nest sites for protection.

Right: In South America, Yellow-rumped Caciques build their nests alongside hanging wasps' nests. The birds live with the insects for protection from enemies. Other animals are not likely to attack a wasps' nest, and both nests look very much alike

Some birds even live with aggressive insects and gain their protection. Black-throated Warblers and Yellow-rumped Caciques nest among the hanging nests of hornets and wasps. Weaver birds build strange nests that can easily be seen by enemies, and so they, too, like to live with wasps. This association helps to protect the birds, but it seems to have little attraction for the insects. The birds often burrow into their breeding places to build nests, and sometimes even eat the insects!

59

Right: An American Robin feeds its young. The young birds sit with their mouths wide open, ready to gobble up as many tasty worms as the parents can find. The chicks depend entirely on the adult birds for nourishment. To get the food, the young have to make the right signals. The parent has the food, but to be fed, the hungry chick must behave in a certain way that the parent bird can recognize. Their behaviour is instinctive, and so it usually succeeds. After about two weeks the chicks get their feathers and start to fly. American Robins breed in the northern United States and Canada and migrate south to the southern U.S.A. and Central America. Their return heralds the arrival of spring in the wintry parts of North America. The American Robin has a full red front, unlike the European Robin which is red only on the upper part of its breast. It is twice the size of the European Robin, and is much more common than the European Robin.

People, too, help to protect young birds. Pigeons, martins, swifts, swallows, weavers, sparrows and starlings use buildings as sites for nesting. In many European countries, the White Stork has been regarded since the Middle Ages as a bird that brings good luck. Because of this superstition, people have always protected the White Stork in Holland and other countries to the east. With the encouragement and protection they receive, White Storks are common in these countries and build nests on the roof tops there. But few White Storks are now to be seen in France, where there is no tradition of protection for storks.

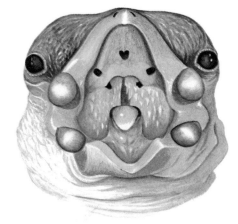

Right: A baby Parrot Finch opens its mouth wide. Baby birds know only one thing: when they are hungry, they gape. The response of the parent is just as instinctive, and it stuffs the open mouth with food until it closes again. This Parrot Finch has a special gape display. The four bright blue spots that show up when the chick opens its mouth produce an irresistible impulse in the parent to feed the chick. The spots also act as a guide for the parent's bill, and they stop the bird from feeding chicks of the wrong species. The spots disappear when the finch is about 5 or 6 weeks old.

SIGNALLING FOR FOOD

Some birds, such as ducks and game birds, hatch from their shells already well grown. They need less looking after than other infant birds and can soon feed themselves and fly. But the chicks of most birds depend entirely on their parents to bring them nourishing food. They must beg and make the right signals to the parents to get the food. This is not difficult; it comes instinctively to the young birds.

New-born Herring Gull chicks peck at a red spot on the lower mandible of the parent bird's bill. This action makes the parent give the food in its bill to the chick. Many birds have young that are born blind and cannot see where the parent's bill is to be found. But as soon as they feel any movement in the nest, the young birds open their mouths and crane their necks in various directions. When their eyes eventually open, they are able to direct their mouths towards the parent.

The young bird's open mouth is a strong signal to the parent bird to stuff it with food. Many infant birds have brightly coloured "gapes", or special markings around their mouths that help to strengthen this signal, as well as to show the parent bird where it has to put the food. The tongue of a baby Horned Lark, for example, is adorned with jet-black spots and bars. These markings disappear when the birds are a few weeks old.

Some birds know which are their young by instinct. Zoologists find it difficult to trick waxbills by exchanging their young for other birds' chicks. But lovebirds learn about their young from their first brood. If their first chicks are taken away and chicks of another species substituted, then the lovebirds will reject any chicks they later have in favour of the substitute species.

Some birds nest in holes where the young are difficult to see. The parent birds respond very much to the sounds the young make. If a recording of the hunger calls of several chicks is played to a pair of Pied Flycatchers with one chick, they will fetch huge quantities of insects, far more than their single chick actually needs.

FAMILY LIFE

Feeding is only one of the many things that a parent bird has to do to rear its young. It has to provide extensive care, starting the moment the baby bird breaks out of its egg. It is then a small, wet and cold thing, and the parent must warm it with its body until it dries out. Then the parent must defend it from its many natural enemies until it is ready to leave the nest. And until the fledgling is ready to live on its own, it must be continually protected so that it can grow into a normal adult bird.

Above: Scientists tried to find out if Arctic Tern chicks peck at colours that remind them of their food. They made models of heads and beaks in various colours, and placed strips of coloured paper in the beaks to look like fish. They found that the chicks' favourite combination was none of those illustrated, but a silver bill with a red "fish", which is exactly the opposite of the real way the chicks feed!

Adult hen Zebra Finch

Young Zebra Finch

To look after its family of young properly, a bird must feel the need to protect them. Protective feelings seem to come naturally to most people when they have to bring up children. But birds must be encouraged to behave in the proper way towards their young, and the young birds give their parents this encouragement.

Because many birds are normally very aggressive towards one another and fight over mates and territories, a young bird must show its parent that it does not want its territory or mate, or the adult bird may attack it. The young birds survive because they usually look different from their parents. Young Zebra Finches have black bills that become red when they grow up. The adult Zebra Finch knows that its young do not present a threat because they have black bills. If a baby bird's black beak is painted red to look like an adult beak, its parents will mistake it for an adult and the young bird will be ignored.

As the young of aggressive birds grow up and start to look more like adult birds, they may start to

"annoy" the parents. The young birds have to keep up their infantile behaviour to show that they are not adults and prevent their parents becoming aggressive towards them. Young Herring Gulls develop a special posture to indicate submission. This posture is the same as one the adults use in courtship. It becomes less effective as the birds get older and more self-sufficient.

Some birds are forced to behave properly towards their offspring. Whenever a Night Heron comes to its nest, it bows to its mate and to its young. The bow is a peace-making gesture, and the young birds recognize their parent by this gesture. If the Night Heron for any reason makes an aggressive gesture instead, then the young birds will attack their own parent!

Nestlings that are very helpless when they are born are in grave danger from the moment they hatch. To protect them, birds often nest in places

Above: Parent birds have to recognize their young if they are to behave in a parental way towards them and protect them. Adult Zebra Finches have scarlet bills, whereas their offspring, for the first few weeks of life, have black bills. If the black bill of a young bird is painted red, the male adult will mistake it for an adult female and will try to court it.
In addition, the black-billed young will be fed by the parents first and the red-billed baby will have to wait for food, no matter how furiously it begs (above right). The paint can soon be removed and the young bird is none the worse for its strange experience. The experiment shows that very simple things, in this case bill colour, easily influence the way in which parent birds behave towards their young. Differences in young birds also serve to inform the adults that the chicks are not competing with them for anything, and so reduce any hostile feelings that they might have.

that are very hard to reach, such as cliff ledges. Large numbers of the birds assemble to breed on these sites. Although crowds of birds tend to attract their enemies, the nests are so hard to get at on the cliffs that the young birds are safe.

Birds that nest together in colonies will come to each other's aid if an enemy approaches. Gulls, terns and skuas will join forces to mob and harry a fox. They will screech at the tops of their voices and swoop down to within a few centimetres of the intruder's face before wheeling away. In desperate situations, some birds will attack and draw blood from humans who venture too close to their nests.

The Golden Plover manages to make an even bigger fool of its enemies. It draws attention from its nest by running away with its wing dragging on the ground as if it were broken. Thinking the plover is easy prey, the marauding animal follows it. But when it is a safe distance from the nest, the plover takes wing and escapes.

Another strange way of protecting a family of young birds is practised by the Purple Sandpiper. This bird lives in the northern wastes and its main enemy is the Arctic Fox. The main food of the fox, however, is rodents. If an Arctic Fox comes close to the nest of a Purple Sandpiper, the bird runs off hunched up and with mincing steps so that it looks like a rodent, thus tempting the fox away from its nest.

NURSERIES

Birds are still in danger after they have left the nests but are not yet fully grown. At this stage, some young birds gather in groups like nurseries or kindergartens. They protect themselves by finding safety in numbers. Young Eider Ducks, flamingos and penguins look after themselves in this way.

Above: Young birds often have to be protected from their parents as well as from their natural enemies. Adult robins are very aggressive birds, and are provoked into instant attack by the sight of the red breast of a rival robin. If the young bird also had a red breast, it would not stand a chance of survival. For their own protection, young robins are dull brown in colour.

Right: The young Night Heron (right) has plumage that camouflages it from view, unlike its parent (left) which can easily be seen. This helps the young bird in situations where danger threatens. An adult heron flees quickly when it is about to be attacked. The young heron is not strong or fast enough to escape in this way, and so it crouches down instead. With luck, the young bird's camouflaged plumage will hide it from the eyes of its enemies.

LEARNING ABOUT LIFE

The way in which a bird behaves affects its whole life. Doing the right thing at the right time means survival. Many of a bird's actions are inborn and it performs them by instinct. But there are important things that a bird must learn as it grows up. Oddly enough, one of the most important things that many young birds must learn is their own identity! Recognizing their own kind does not come naturally to them, strange as it may seem to us.

Ever since Noah's Ark, people have sorted animals into different kinds, two by two. The animals themselves have been doing this for as long as they have lived in the world. They easily sort themselves out and breed pair by pair. Yet although many species of birds look very much alike, birds very rarely interbreed with different birds.

Some birds can recognize their own kind naturally. Cuckoos and other parasite birds never see their parents, yet they know exactly what kind of mate they must select later in life to be able to breed. But many birds go through a critical stage when they have to learn who they are. Whatever they learn at this time is permanent – it cannot be undone afterwards. It is called *imprinting*.

IMPRINTING

Ducklings and goslings remain in the egg for a long time, and are well developed when they hatch. They have feathers and can walk. One of their first

Above: A young duckling clambers over an obstacle to keep up with a model of its parent. When ducklings hatch, they instinctively follow the parents, who lead them away from the nest to the water. During the first two days of their lives, they absorb the characteristics of the parent, and become attached to them. If the new-born duckling has to struggle to follow its parents, then the attachment formed is all the stronger for its struggle. Zoologists made young ducklings climb over hurdles to follow a model of their parent. They found that the ducklings that had to struggle originally were more persistent in trying to follow the model. Forming this attachment is called *imprinting*. It is a learning process and cannot be undone.

Left: An Eider Duck leads her brood of ducklings to open water. Normally the ducklings become imprinted on their parents and follow them around. A line of ducklings straggling along behind a duck on a lake is a common sight. But if the ducklings are hatched artificially and brought up without their natural parents, they will attach themselves to a foster parent, which may even be a human being. The ducklings will then follow their human "parent" everywhere. When they grow up, they will direct all their relationships towards humans instead of towards ducks! But normal imprinting is valuable because it keeps the birds in the company of their own kind.

actions is to follow their parents. The adult birds lead them away from the nest to open water. The desire to follow is so strong that if the ducklings are deprived of their parents and hand-reared, they will follow any moving object, even a human being!

During these first few hours, the young bird absorbs the features of the "parent", whether it is a real parent, or a foster parent such as another bird or a human being. It learns that it is the same creature as this "parent". When it grows up, it will seek the company of those resembling this "parent" and try to mate with them. This imprinting of an identity cannot be reversed. If the "parent" it follows when young is not its real parent, then the bird will go through life thinking it is some other bird or animal.

Imprinting occurs early in life. In Mallard Ducks, it is strongest when the bird is between 13 and 16 hours old. By 24 hours later, imprinting has almost finished. If a duckling is forced to accept a strange mother during its first two days of life, then it will never learn to live with its own kind. If a farmer has to rear a clutch of goslings by hand, then the goslings will prefer humans for company to other geese.

Such mistakes of identity are rare, however, and most birds that learn by imprinting identify with their own parents. This keeps many different kinds of birds from disappearing from the world, because these birds will not interbreed with other kinds of birds. The birds look for reminders of their parents when they choose a mate. Domestic pigeons come in all colours, but they look for mates that resemble their parents (and therefore resemble themselves). In this way, certain varieties of birds are maintained and do not die out.

Below: Bird fanciers often use Bengalese Finches as foster parents to rear young birds of other species. If the young bird is with the Bengalese Finch when it is between 30 and 40 days old, then it will come to think that it is a Bengalese Finch. It will prefer the company of Bengalese Finches, even if it can live with its own kind. If young male Zebra Finches are reared by a female Bengalese Finch (top), they will court female Bengalese Finches when they grow up (bottom). They will do this even if they have an opportunity to mate with female Zebra Finches. Bird fanciers have to be careful about using foster parents, because birds raised in this way will never be able to breed. The 35th day of life is very critical for a Zebra Finch if it is to learn which parent is which. When the brood of young finches is between 35 and 40 days old, the male parent chases them away from the home. His hostility at this time seems to teach the young males that they must court females later in life.

Left: A male Oregon Junco sings with a simple trill. Oregon Juncos that are reared by hand from the egg and kept from hearing the song of their fellow wild birds sing much more inventively. These deprived juncos are capable of singing some elaborate song patterns. But if the deprived birds later hear the simple song of the wild males, they will lose their musical ability. They forget their elaborate songs and learn instead the simple trill of their wild kind. The Song Sparrow is related to the Oregon Junco. It has a more complicated and tuneful song, but it does not have to learn it. Young Arizona Juncos develop songs on hearing other birds sing. But they do not copy the other birds in any way and so cannot learn from them. The other song merely serves to put these juncos in an inventive singing mood.

A bird does not only learn what it looks like. Wood Ducks nest in holes and the parent has to entice the young out of the holes after they hatch. The ducklings become imprinted to the calls of the parent, and later associate with birds that call in the same way. Rails, Moorhens and Coots also become imprinted to calls.

SINGING LESSONS

Singing does not always come naturally to birds, and many have to learn to sing. Brood parasites like the cuckoo develop their song without being taught by others of their own kind. But these birds are on their own right from the very start of life and do not even need imprinting to help gain their own identity.

Right: The male White-crowned Sparrow learns its song during the first hundred days of its life before it can actually sing. It stores up the information it needs by listening to the song of other male White-crowned Sparrows. If it does not hear its fellow males singing at this early stage of its life, then the bird will produce an incorrect song later in its life. As the birds learn to sing, differences in song occur between different populations of White-crowned Sparrows. Like human dialects, the farther apart the populations, the greater are the differences in song.

Below: The male Marsh Warbler (left) and the male Yellow-breasted Chat. Birds learning to sing often pick up phrases from other different birds in composing their own songs. The Marsh Warbler has been heard to mimic 39 other species of birds. Yellow-breasted Chats are exceptional North American mimics. Together with the Common Jay, the Marsh Warbler is the best mimic in Britain. The best in North America is the Mockingbird.

Many birds need singing lessons to get the notes of their song right. The young birds will try to sing by instinct, but the results are not very tuneful. They need to hear other birds of their own kind singing before they can sing properly.

Zoologists have studied the songs of chaffinches. Young chaffinches reared by hand and kept from their fellows developed a song that was the right length and had the right number of notes. But they did not phrase the song correctly. The young go through two sensitive periods when they learn the details from listening to the song of fully-grown birds. The first lesson takes place when the young bird is in the nest or has just left it. The second lesson is during the following spring, when it can practise with other chaffinches.

Not all birds learn to sing by imitation. Some birds are merely put into a singing mood by hearing others sing. They do not copy the others, but rely on their own inventiveness. In other cases, the birds are very inventive if left to their own devices. But when they hear the song of their own kind, they stop trying to make up a song, and learn the proper one.

Most songs seem to be learned from other birds in the same region, so it is not surprising that some birds develop local "dialects", just as human beings do. The dialect is handed down to the young birds, who imitate it. Songs in the local dialect may get a better response from the birds in the region than songs in another dialect.

Human Voice

you make me laugh

mynah bird

Above: Spectrograms are visual records of bird calls. They show how the pitch of the notes in a call changes. The spectrograms above show the sentence "You make me laugh" as spoken by a human voice and by a mynah bird. The striking similarity of the two indicates that the bird made a remarkable imitation of the human voice. Parrots often learn that certain sounds go with certain events, and they can remember them and mimic them. Parrots have been known to say "Hello" whenever a telephone rings.

As many birds learn to sing by imitating adult birds, it is not surprising that some birds pick up the song of other kinds of birds. The Robin Chat of Africa sometimes produces a song that is made up entirely of phrases from other birds. The Mockingbird of America has been heard to imitate 55 other birds in the space of an hour! In the wild, birds may mimic other birds, or even the cries of preying animals, in order to make a diversion and attract an intruder away from its nest, or to frighten it off.

TALKING BIRDS

Some birds are so good at imitations that they can even mimic the human voice. Talking birds such as parrots and mynah birds often "talk" when they are alone, perhaps in an effort to bring their owners to them. They cannot understand the meaning of the words they utter so well. But they do associate sounds with events. A parrot can learn to say "Goodbye" when people leave a room. It may then start to say "Goodbye" when people that it dislikes are in the room, presumably to try and get rid of them!

MIGRATION

For thousands of years, people have watched birds gather together as the winter or summer approaches and fly off in huge flocks. We often envy their ability to fly away from a cold winter. If we live in hot climates, we may be jealous of the way birds can leave for cooler areas to breed while we swelter in their absence.

Complete populations of certain birds will migrate north or south every year. Giant Petrels and many albatrosses that nest on lonely islands in the southern oceans migrate all the way round the world between their breeding seasons, blown by the Roaring Forties and other winds in that hemisphere.

Migration helps birds to survive. They can follow good weather. Insect eaters feast on the multitudes of insects that can be found in the north during the spring and summer. But when winter approaches and the harsh weather starts to make food scarce, the bird migrates south to more hospitable regions.

LONG DISTANCE TRAVELLERS

Some birds migrate fantastic distances, so far that the world hardly seems big enough for them. Arctic Terns probably hold the record. They breed every summer as near to the North Pole as you can get on land – about 800 km away. Then they migrate down the Atlantic coasts of Europe and Africa to the Antarctic Circle and back every year, making a round trip of nearly 60,000 km! These birds follow the sun as they migrate back and forth from pole to pole, and they probably see more daylight during their lives than any other creature in the world.

Other great travellers are the Pacific Golden Plover, which flies non-stop across 3,200 km of ocean twice a year, and the little Ruby-throated Humming-bird, which makes a non-stop trip of 800 to 1,600 km across the Gulf of Mexico.

KEEPING TRACK OF BIRDS

Bird watchers in bird observatories look out for flocks of migrating birds every year. They time them, note which birds are taking part in the migration, and watch to see how the weather affects the flocks.

Below: The Slender-billed Shearwater has one of the longest migration routes of any bird. It breeds on the islands in Bass Strait between Tasmania and Australia. Then the birds migrate in a great circle completely around the Pacific Ocean. The journey takes 3 or 4 years, and the shearwater usually returns to the island where it was reared to raise its own young.

breeding area ▬▬▬
migration route ▬▬▬

In many countries, special ringing units put marked bands or rings around birds' legs before they migrate. Anyone seeing a ringed bird should try to note the information on the ring and send it back to the ringing unit with a record of where and when the bird was seen. In this way, scientists find out exactly what routes migrating birds follow and how long their journeys take.

Radar has helped us to track flocks of birds, just as it helps airport traffic controllers to keep a watch on their aircraft. It has shown that many flocks of migrating birds fly at great heights of 1,000 m or more. These high flights are often different from the low-flying bird movements that bird watchers see from the ground. It is possible that the low-flying birds have become lost from the main high-flying flock. Another advantage of using radar is that it can be used at night, for many birds migrate under cover of darkness to escape their enemies.

Satellites orbiting round the Earth in space are keeping watch on the migration of large animals such as the elk. The animal carries a radio transmitter which continuously broadcasts its position to the satellite. One day, the transmitters may be made small enough to fix to a bird like a ring, and then we shall be able to follow a migrating bird all the time.

FINDING THE WAY

A bird gets "itchy wings" and begins to feel the need to move as the days get shorter at the end of its breeding season. It has spent the summer rearing its young at the breeding grounds, and they are now old enough to start to look after themselves. The shortening days change the balance of hormone chemicals in the bird's body. This change makes the bird feed ravenously. It puts on weight – valuable fat which will give the bird fuel for its long migration flight. Suddenly it is time to go. The birds gather in a great wheeling, twittering flock in the sky and off they fly towards the warm wintering grounds. It is a thrilling sight.

No-one really knows exactly how birds fly such vast distances without ever getting lost. Many birds have a homing ability, and if released a long way from home, will find their way back. This is not exactly the same as migration, but the homing ability is well developed in migrating birds. One bird flew home 5,000 km across the Atlantic Ocean. It took only 12½ days, for the bird knew exactly where it was going.

Right: The Golden Plover is one of the world's great travellers. The western variety, the Pacific Golden Plover, breeds in the far north of Alaska and Siberia. To migrate, it wings its way non-stop across 3,200 km of the Pacific Ocean to Hawaii. It may then carry on farther south. The eastern variety makes an even longer journey. It breeds across northern Canada. As winter approaches, the adult birds migrate to their winter home in South America. They make a 3,800 km journey over Labrador, Newfoundland and the Atlantic Ocean. The young birds do not attempt the ocean crossing, but fly down the middle of America instead. But all the birds come back overland. The returning plovers use the Mississippi Flyway for part of their route. This extends along the Mississippi River and includes the states that lie along the river. It is one of four flyways used by birds in the United States. The Central Flyway lies between Montana and the Dakotas and due south. The Atlantic Flyway and Pacific Flyway lie along the east and west coasts of the country.

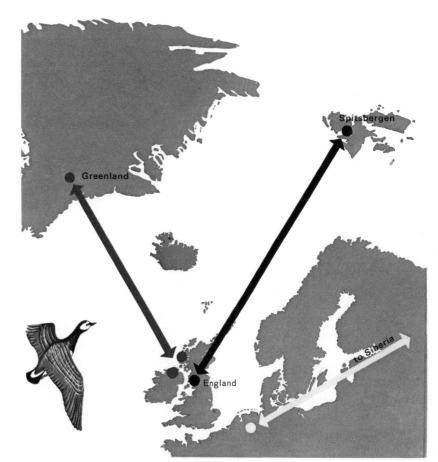

Western race—summer area
Eastern race—summer area
////// Eastern race—winter area
——— Flight path of Western race to winter area
——— Flight path of adult Eastern birds on return journey
– – – Flight path of young Eastern birds on return journey
▬▬▬ Flight path of adult Eastern birds on outward journey
▬ ▬ ▬ Flight path of young Eastern birds on outward journey

Right: Barnacle Geese have various breeding areas. From Holland they go to Siberia, from the Solway Firth in Scotland to Spitsbergen, and from other parts of Scotland and Ireland to Greenland. This information was obtained by ringing them. Barnacle Geese got their name during the Middle Ages, when people knew nothing of the northern lands where they breed. It was popularly believed that they hatched from barnacles!

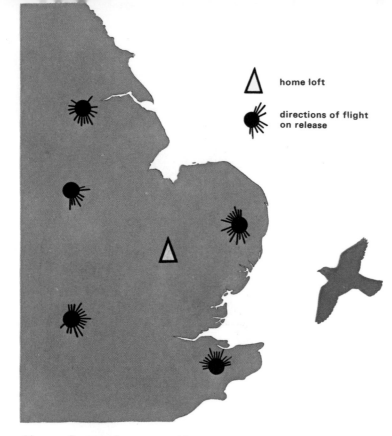

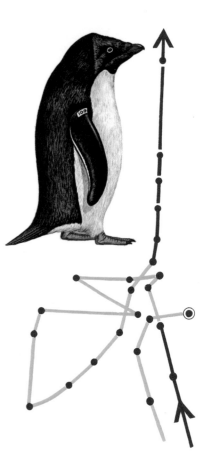

Above: Racing pigeons are able to navigate and find their way home wherever they may be. The map shows the directions that some birds took on being released from various places up to about 200 km from their loft. None of the pigeons flew in the opposite direction to the loft, and most began to fly straight towards it. It is possible that the pigeon may be able to navigate from the position of the sun in the sky. But the pigeon's complete navigation method is probably much more complicated than this.

△ home loft

✹ directions of flight on release

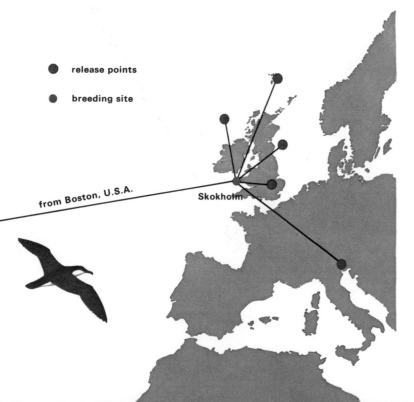

● release points

● breeding site

from Boston, U.S.A.

Skokholm

Left: Most homing birds lose their homing ability if they are taken too far from home. But Manx Shearwaters find their way back over immense distances. Several shearwaters were taken from the island of Skokholm, a bird sanctuary off the coast of Wales. They were released in various parts of Europe, and one was taken across the Atlantic Ocean to Boston. All the birds found their way back to the island in a short time. The bird from Boston took only $12\frac{1}{2}$ days to make its journey of 5,000 km! The bird's speedy return indicated that it must have known exactly where to go.

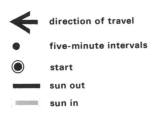

←	direction of travel
●	five-minute intervals
◉	start
▬	sun out
▬	sun in

Left: An Adélie Penguin, trying to find its way on a field of ice where everything looks the same, navigates by the sun. The black dots show its position every 5 minutes. When the sun was out, it moved purposefully over the ice in a straight line (black lines). But when the sun went in, it seemed to lose its way and wandered about aimlessly in all directions (blue lines). But as soon as the sun reappeared, the penguin set off in a straight line again.

Birds seem to be able to navigate by somehow observing the position of the sun and pattern of the stars, because migrating birds get lost if it is cloudy. Each migrating bird seems to have an inborn ability to fix its position and fly on a set course by the sun and stars. Human navigators do so as well, but they need a sextant to observe the position of the sun and stars in the sky, and an accurate chronometer to find out the exact time for their calculations. Birds have an inborn biological clock and seem to know the exact time at any instant. Somehow, without using instruments or tables as we have to, they can navigate accurately over the globe.

Birds can alter course if they get blown off-route by side winds. They may estimate the distance that they are drifting off-course by watching landmarks, islands or cloud formations overhead, or from the direction in which the wind blows against their feathers.

It is possible to fool migrating birds. Zoologists captured some young crows that were half-way through a migration flight to the north. They moved them a long way to the west and released them. Many flew on as if nothing had happened, and so ended up a long way to the west of their breeding grounds. This experiment was also tried with migrating starlings. The young birds were fooled, but the older birds who had migrated before turned up in their usual winter quarters.

Migration and navigation are still great mysteries to us. There is still a great deal to be discovered about this amazing aspect of bird behaviour.

Right: Birds were captured making a stop at a bird sanctuary at Rossiten or Rybachi, near Kaliningrad in Russia, during their spring migration. The birds, young Hooded Crows, were taken 750 km west to Flensburg in Germany. There they were ringed and released. Many of the birds were later recaptured a long way west of their summer homes. They had continued their journey in the directions they would have followed had they been leaving Rossiten after their stop-over.

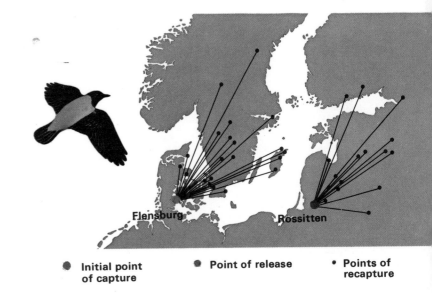

Flensburg   Rossitten

| ● | Initial point of capture | ● | Point of release | • | Points of recapture |

INDEX

Figures in bold type refer to illustrations and captions